Lessons from Lockport

Lessons from Lockport
Dispatches from the Great American Divide

JIM SHULTZ

excelsior editions
State University of New York Press
Albany, New York

Cover photo by Lee Williams.

Published by State University of New York Press, Albany

© 2025 State University of New York

All rights reserved

Printed in the United States of America

No part of this book may be used or reproduced in any manner whatsoever without written permission. No part of this book may be stored in a retrieval system or transmitted in any form or by any means including electronic, electrostatic, magnetic tape, mechanical, photocopying, recording, or otherwise without the prior permission in writing of the publisher.

Links to third-party websites are provided as a convenience and for informational purposes only. They do not constitute an endorsement or an approval of any of the products, services, or opinions of the organization, companies, or individuals. SUNY Press bears no responsibility for the accuracy, legality, or content of a URL, the external website, or for that of subsequent websites.

EU GPSR Authorised Representative:
Logos Europe, 9 rue Nicolas Poussin, 17000, La Rochelle, France
contact@logoseurope.eu

Excelsior Editions is an imprint of State University of New York Press

For information, contact State University of New York Press, Albany, NY
www.sunypress.edu

Library of Congress Cataloging-in-Publication Data

Name: Shultz, Jim, author.
Title: Lessons from Lockport : dispatches from the great American divide / Jim Shultz.
Description: Albany : State University of New York Press, [2025] | Series: Excelsior editions | Includes bibliographical references and index.
Identifiers: LCCN 2024042809 | ISBN 9798855802337 (pbk. : alk. paper) | ISBN 9798855802320 (ebook)
Subjects: LCSH: Shultz, Jim. | Conservatives—New York (State)—Lockport—Attitudes. | Community activists—New York (State)—Lockport—Biography. | Lockport (N.Y.)—Social conditions. | Lockport (N.Y.)—Politics and government. | Lockport (N.Y.)—Social life and customs. | Lockport (N.Y.)—Biography.
Classification: LCC F129.L765 S38 2025 | DDC 974.7/98044092 [B]—dc23/eng/20250206
LC record available at https://lccn.loc.gov/2024042809

*For Isabella and Elena,
the two coolest Lockportians I know.*

Contents

Acknowledgments	ix
Prologue	xi
1. The Town and the Writer	1
2. Spy Cameras in the Schools	25
3. Black in Lockport	51
4. A Rebellion against Renewable Power	75
5. A Castle of Old School Corruption	101
6. Conversations with My Neighbors	125
Conclusion	167
Notes	175
About the Author	183
Index	185

Acknowledgments

My first thanks go to the people of Lockport. I was a stranger in a strange land, and you took me in. What a gift you have given me at this stage in my life: to be near family in a good small town. Thank you especially to my readers here. I have enjoyed writing for you and have learned so much from you. I hope you enjoy the book.

Many thanks to all the kind people who let me interview them for this book and for my articles that preceded it. This includes, most especially, Margaret Darroch, Mindy Vizscarra, Jayde McDonald, Will King, Kandyce Cauley, Mark Sanders, Michael Nolan, Phil Barnes, Markus Campbell, Flora Hawkins, Bob Confer, Michelle Roman, Gene Baes, Jon Hotaling, and Kristi Winquist.

A number of friends generously agreed to look at drafts of different pieces of the book and give me their very helpful feedback. This includes Stefanie Coyle, Chris Proctor, Randy Atwater, Joe Caves, Jude McCartin, Maryann O'Sullivan, Connor Hoffman, and Mark Scheer.

Connor and Mark, along with Benjamin Joe, Tim Fenster, Phil Gambini, and Jim Heaney, have also served as dedicated Western New York journalists, and the reporting of each of them has been deeply helpful to my understanding of so many complicated stories.

Two editors and friends have had a huge impact on my writing about Lockport and this special corner of New York. Joyce Miles at the *Lockport Union-Sun & Journal* gave me my column in the paper, has been a wonderful editor to work with for nearly seven years, and on top of all that let me interview her for this book and offered very helpful comments on the draft. That is a lot of journalistic kinship for which I am deeply grateful. Thanks as well to Matt Seaton, who has been my editor at *New*

York Review. Through the articles I wrote for NYR he helped shape my understanding of how to present these stories to a national audience. He also gave me some insightful early advice, "Stop covering Lockport like you are an astronaut visiting Mars."

Thank you to the staff at SUNY Press for their support for this book and their hard work getting it into readers' hands.

Lastly, thank you to my family. Michael and Elly, thank you for bringing us here to Lockport. Isabella and Elena, living across the street from the two of you is absolutely the best thing about living here. Lynn and Mariana, thank you for being my companions on the great Lockport adventure. Lola the dog, you've been very patient. Let's go for a walk in the woods and chase sticks.

Prologue

The bar was packed. It was a Saturday night in late Spring and the Western New York crowd was excited to be out after a long winter. It was a place where pickups in the parking lot were plentiful, and a rock and roll band on stage belted out covers from the 1970s, 80s, and 90s.

"Hey, are you that guy who writes for the newspaper?"

The man with the dark shaggy hair and a beard to match showed up suddenly at my side. I got asked this question so often at this point that I had a standard response at the ready. "Do you like that guy who writes for the paper?" This always left room open for a denial if it seemed needed. That night though, two drinks in, I just went for a straight-up admission. "Yes I am."

"I disagree with almost everything you write. But I think you are honest."

That began a ten-minute soliloquy that ran through the misdeeds of Joe Biden, the general decline of the nation, and assorted complaints about the sins that Democrats and liberals were inflicting on the country. I listened. When he hit his grievances over inflation I couldn't disagree with his anger. "I'm a plumber. I make $29 an hour and I can't afford anything anymore," he told me.

Then he landed on an issue that took me aback. "The transgenders! They are everywhere! They are shoving it down our throats." I decided that I would dig a little deeper on this topic. In this part of New York State people swapping gender are not exactly something you run into much.

"Wait, how do transgender people affect your life in any way at all?" I asked him.

"They are all over. They are all over the mainstream media. It's all we hear about now."

I added a note to my list of political lessons gleaned from living in this small town. Clever right-wing pundits—who had moved on from the great threat to Dr. Seuss—had now made all things transgender their new target for attack. They had also apparently scored a double victory. Not only did the issue serve up a fresh subject of culture war outrage to boost their viewership, but it also left those viewers with the impression that it was transgender people making all the noise rather than the people attacking them.

Soon afterward my conversation companion moved on amicably, and I turned my attention back to my family, my drink, and the band.

It wasn't long before another man spotted me, this time from the other side of the bar. He was big, built like one of the trucks out back. His hair was close cropped, and he had a huge bushy brown beard. The look he gave me was intense, and he was quickly heading in my direction through the crowd. He came so close to my face that he didn't have to raise his voice by much for me to hear him over a loud Rolling Stones cover. He leaned in, grabbed my hand, and told me, "I love everything you write man." Then he walked on without any further introduction or comment.

"Who are these people?" Ever since the first rise of Donald Trump to the center of the nation's politics, this is the question that has been asked in liberal corners all across the country. What is going on in small town and rural America that people elsewhere don't understand? What has driven a good portion of the country's working class into the political arms of a fast-talking, billionaire real estate mogul from New York City? These questions have been dissected by pollsters, analyzed by pundits, and written about at length in one book after another. But still, almost a decade later, the answer seems unsettled.

The dividing of America into sheltered enclaves of the like-minded has been written about a lot in recent years. Liberals live with liberals in the big cities along the coasts and in affluent suburbs. Conservatives have hunkered down with conservatives in the small towns and wide-open rural spaces in between. We increasingly live our lives in comfortable echo chambers of political and social compatibility, not only in the media we consume but in the neighbors who surround us.

I do not have that problem.

The City of Lockport, New York (population 20,420), is a small working-class city in the conservative northwest corner of the state near the

Canadian border. The city is the official seat of Niagara County, a sparsely populated rectangle of land with a world-famous waterfall at its western edge and small towns and farms dotted across the rest of it. The county has also reliably supported Donald Trump in every election, by double digits.

Lockport was born two centuries ago from the digging of the Erie Canal—that historic waterway and one-time engine of commerce that still meanders gently through the city's center. Even after the Canal's decline as a commercial hub, the city continued to be an industrial powerhouse through most of the 1900s. Lockport was home to a giant General Motors plant that employed thousands of people and paid union wages.

That came to a swift end in the early 1990s under the blade of a massive GM downsizing and made Lockport emblematic of many communities in postindustrial economic decline. It is small towns and farming communities like these, throughout the country, that have set alight the conservative populist politics altering the nation. Here it is possible to get a close-up view of why.

Lockport was a very strange place for me to move to on the eve of my sixtieth birthday. I lived my first forty years in California, including two decades in the liberal epicenter of the Bay Area. I lived for twenty years after that in the Andean foothills of Bolivia, during its years of leftist political revolution. Then, in the summer of 2017, I suddenly found myself back once again in the United States, six months into Donald Trump's presidency, and in a county that had voted for him by a wide margin.

The other unexpected thing that followed was my becoming a weekly opinion columnist for the town's 200-year-old daily newspaper, the venerable *Lockport Union-Sun & Journal*, and becoming the county's resident provocative liberal writer.

The path that brought our family from rural Bolivia to Lockport required an unusual chain of events. Thirty years earlier I had to meet and marry a wonderful young woman from Buffalo, Lynn Nesselbush. We had to spend our first year of marriage volunteering in a Bolivian orphanage and coming home with a five-year-old adopted daughter, Elizabeth. Then Elizabeth had to move to the US for college, take a job afterward in Buffalo, walk into the Lockport Applebee's one night and meet her future husband, Michael. Lastly they had to call us on New Year's Day 2017 to tell us we were going to be grandparents.

It was the grandchild that clinched it. That next summer we left Bolivia with our youngest daughter, Mariana, and with our dog Lola. We set off on what was supposed to be a six-month adventure, returning to Bolivia as soon as winter arrived. That was the plan. Instead we stayed.

In the field of public opinion research there are two primary tools. One is polling, the practice of asking a random sample of people what they think about things such as who the president should be or what beer they like. The other tool is the focus group. This involves putting together a small random group of people in a room together and letting them talk about something such as who the president should be or what beer they like. The goal with a focus group is not mathematical extrapolation but the chance to hear how people talk about things. The insight it offers is different and deeper.

In Lockport I live daily in a real-world focus group filled with a lot of people who have a very different life experience than mine and because of that a very different view of the world. I publish columns on everything from guns and immigration to the misdeeds of local officials. I also began posting those columns to a local Facebook group that included pretty much everyone in Lockport. It did not take long to start hearing from people about what I was writing.

On the street, in line at the store, in playgrounds, in bars and beyond, I began to find myself in conversations about everything from taxes to Trump, often with people who didn't precisely agree with what I had written. On Facebook some of my articles would spark whole community debates.

What I began to receive was a valuable political education about how people think in conservative working-class and rural America. That education offered insight into how the same issues riling up the nation played out here, up close.

Later I began sharing stories from here with a national audience. I wrote articles for the *New York Times* and *New York Review*. This included a long article in *NYR* titled, "A Liberal in Trumpland." In it I wrote: "There are reasons that people think what they think and feel what they feel and if we ever hope to find common ground, we need to find a way to hear them. And it might be while waiting on line at the drug store."

I have come to believe that the story that captures this time in America most is the story from the Buddha about three blind men and an elephant. A king orders the men to touch what is in front of them and say what it is. One grabs the tail and says it's a snake. Another touches the leg and declares it to be a large tree. The third touches its side and insists it is a giant boulder. Each has a piece of the truth but none have the actual truth. They get into a fight over who is right.

This feels like the story of America right now. We have fallen into an epidemic of certainty. Doubt is considered weakness. Actually listening to anyone with a differing point of view is heresy. Like the blind men, none of us have a monopoly on truth but our battles are bringing democracy to the breaking point.

By every imaginable stereotype, I belong in a place like Berkeley or Brooklyn, not here. I became an activist at fourteen. I was a teenager in Richard Nixon's hometown while he was president. I volunteered for his anti–Vietnam War opponent, Senator George McGovern. I studied political science at UC Berkeley, then public administration at Harvard. I lived in San Francisco and worked for twenty years as a public interest advocate in California politics. I helped organize advocacy campaigns for universal health care, for immigrant rights, and for an end to US funding for the wars in Central America. In Bolivia I reported from the front lines of leftist political uprisings. I founded an organization called the Democracy Center and have spent more than three decades supporting the work of social justice and environmental activists on five continents.

Yet here I landed, in Lockport.

Lessons from Lockport is a set of stories that offer a close-up look at a part of America that is often misunderstood. These stories are about the same issues we struggle over as a nation—about who the economy is leaving behind, race and identity, public safety and policing, how to protect our environment, public corruption, and about what it means to be a community. That close-up view offers some valuable insight for the country as a whole.

This is not my first time living in and writing about a place and culture not my own. During the nineteen years that my family and I lived in Bolivia I was also an outsider who wrote about what I saw and what lessons that had to the wider world. This included dozens of major articles, a widely read blog, and two full-length books. I wrote especially about the real-world impacts of globalization, the most well-known being my writing about the Cochabamba Water War.

Moving to Lockport after twenty years abroad felt like moving to a new culture once again. I am fortunate here to have my own views on things challenged all the time. I have real conversations with people like the woman who works the register at the local produce store and a young farmer I see each week at the community market. It also happens on occasion in bars. I have traveled to the other side of the elephant, and this book is written from a hundred moments like these strung together.

Barbara Kingsolver recently wrote a novel set in her native Appalachia. She explained that she hoped it would be a mirror for the people who live there and a window for those who do not. That is my hope here as well, not about the place where I was born, but instead one that adopted me late in life.

Welcome to Western New York.

Jim Shultz
Lockport, January 2025

Chapter One

The Town and the Writer

If you choose the right route into Lockport from the south, it is possible to arrive here solely on streets named after Republican presidents. A left turn off Lincoln Avenue will put you on to Nixon Place. Then, in a shortcut through history, you can travel along Hoover Parkway directly to Eisenhower Drive, without any pesky Democratic FDR or Truman in between. If you are willing to make a more circuitous approach you can also add on two blocks' worth of Harding and Coolidge. There is a Roosevelt Drive farther along, but I am reasonably sure that it is named for Theodore the Republican, not Franklin the Democrat.

Lockport's history, which is abundant, drips with old-school Republicanism. Barry Goldwater's 1964 vice-presidential running mate, William E. Miller, was the local GOP Congressman here and a graduate of Lockport High School. It has long been the kind of community where political power rested with a handful of White men of the local establishment, who owned the local businesses, held status in local congregations, lived in the biggest houses, and inhabited its positions of public authority. It is also a place that has spawned its share of other local celebrities, including a NASA astronaut and the prolific writer, Joyce Carol Oates.

But more recently something has changed. An old guard still controls much of the local political power, but the spiritual mantle of conservative politics has been passed elsewhere. No longer is its epicenter affluent families in mansions who practiced the staid politics of the gentry and generally respected both facts and the norms of democratic rule.

Today the more visible and loud conservatism is of the populist variety. It is found most vocally among the white working-class families who live on different streets than the affluent and who often express themselves in the coarse anger of the time we live in. A good many of them love Donald Trump deeply and love what he stands for.

The City of Lockport is a creation of two waves of local history in which prosperity first boomed and then crashed.

The first was the construction of the Erie Canal across New York State from Albany to Buffalo. Built in the first half of the 1820s, the Canal was one of the most impressive engineering feats of its time. Constructed four decades before Alfred Nobel invented dynamite, a good portion of its route had to be carved out of dense rock using nothing but gunpowder and hard labor. That labor came mostly from the backs of migrant men from Ireland and Black men who traveled west from New York City.

The Canal stretches for 363 miles from one end to the other. Its opening in 1825 created the first shipping connection from Chicago and the Great Lakes all the way to New York City via the Hudson River. Barges carrying staples of grain, lumber, and flour were famously towed along by ropes tied to mules who walked at a slow pace on a path set to the side. If a song made popular in the early 1900s is to be believed, at least one of the mules was named Sal.

As the Canal's route ran its last miles westward before meeting up with Lake Erie, 1820s engineers had a major problem to solve. They had to come up with a way to lift and lower the barges up and down the same natural fifty-foot escarpment that created Niagara Falls. Their solution was to construct a set of large wooden locks that filled with water and lifted and lowered the boats like elevators. The last of these, and the most impressive, was the Flight of Five in Lockport.

The Canal and the locks gave birth to a small city of outsized creativity in a place that not long ago had been just a wide spot in the woods. The boatmen waiting for their turn to take their barges through the locks needed stores for supplies, rooms to stay the night, and bars to pass the time. The new city took its name from the locks, and the new prosperity they generated lasted for decades.

Over time, however, the Erie Canal's commercial dominance took one direct hit after another from leaps in technology. First came the trains, which offered a faster and cheaper means of moving freight. Local lore here is that the city's famous upside-down railroad bridge over the canal was constructed with all its metal framing on the underside to limit the height of the competing barges. Then came the interstate highway system, which was faster and cheaper still. The waterway shipping that was left was taken over in the late 1950s by a more modern and wider route built through the Saint Lawrence Seaway to the north in Canada.

By the time my family arrived in Lockport in 2017 the Canal had been long sidelined to the status of recreational waterway and tourist attraction. But it had once made the city beside it a place of great wealth, especially for a few.

This same pattern of economic bonanza and crash repeated itself here in the 1900s. In 1910 a local inventor named Herbert Harrison patented and began manufacturing the honeycombed radiator. It was soon adopted by an infant automobile industry as the standard for cooling car engines. The Harrison Radiator Company began with a bustling factory right in Lockport's downtown.[1] By the late 1920s it was producing more than two million automobile and truck radiators a year and continued to do so for decades. Today a good number of the obituaries in the local paper still include some reference to "worked for the Harrison Radiator Company for thirty years." Later, through a series of sales and mergers, the company became a part of General Motors.

GM eventually moved operations to a much larger factory on the outskirts of the city. In the GM plant's heyday of the 1960s, 1970s, and 1980s, it employed more than ten thousand well-paid union workers. If you drove a GM car or truck anytime up until the early 1990s there is a good chance your radiator was manufactured here in Lockport. Graduates from Lockport High School, boys and girls alike, had the option of old-school, lifetime employment with a union wage and a pension (though older members of the community here will tell you the jobs went mostly to people with connections at the plant). GM helped grow Lockport into a thriving small city.

The boom ended abruptly over the Christmas holiday in 1991 when GM announced closures at twenty-one plants nationwide, Lockport's among them.[2] The city was economically gutted overnight. It has still never fully recovered. The plant is down to fifteen hundred workers now, and many stores and offices along Main Street still lie vacant. My first Lockport haircut was from a man named Todd who told me that he used to make twice as much working on the GM assembly line. Today, one in six people here live below the poverty line and a good many others live right on the margin.[3]

This shared sense of loss, and nostalgia for a time when opportunity for working people was more certain, has a good deal to do with the politics of America in our time. It is also built firmly into the collective DNA of this conservative corner of Western New York and of Lockport. The remnants of that lost prosperity are all over town.

At one edge of the city sits the red brick ruins of Union Station. Constructed in 1889, it was once an elegant train depot that offered regular service to Niagara Falls, Buffalo, and Rochester. Today its crumbling remains sit behind a falling chain link fence and are covered in weeds. A few blocks away, a nondescript Walgreens store sits on the site of what used to be a bustling street car depot, which dispatched trolleys across the city and outward to places like Olcott, a tiny hamlet on the shore of Lake Ontario that was itself once a thriving summer tourist resort.

In decades past, Lockport's downtown possessed an opera house, two large department stores, blocks of elegant buildings constructed in the late 1800s, and some of the original structures erected in the days of the Canal's opening. Much of that was demolished through an infamous Urban Renewal campaign in the 1960s and 70s. That so-called renewal of the city also took out whole neighborhoods occupied mostly by the city's Black residents and recently arrived Italians. Classic old architecture dating back a century was replaced with short, squat storefronts and offices devoid of all character.

Amidst the demolitions there have also been successful preservation efforts here as well. The jewel among these is the beautiful Palace Theater on Main Street, opened in 1925 and later rescued and renovated by a citizen nonprofit group. Today it is a venue for everything from community musicals to my granddaughters' dance recital.

After the Erie Canal was first built, innovative local manufacturers used diverted water to power a whole assortment of factories and mills. One of them, Birdsill Holly Jr., patented the fire hydrant and manufactured it here. Other manufacturing operations followed and eventually spread beyond the Canal and became factories of a very different kind. Run by corporations like the United Paperboard Company and others, they left the water and the land adjacent to it laden with deadly contaminants including PCBs and lead. A few blocks from the city center sits a contaminated Environmental Protection Agency Superfund site, Eighteen Mile Creek.[4] For some, it felt like Lockport's own version of Love Canal, the notorious toxic waste site just a half hour's drive away in Niagara Falls.

One evening during my first year here I attended an EPA informational forum about the Superfund site. I listened as one family after another told terrible stories of mothers, fathers, siblings, children, and pets diagnosed with cancer, some of whom had died. They blamed it on the contamination. The EPA officials warned them not to let their children go barefoot in their yards and not to let them bring their shoes in the house. "Are you serious?" said one angry father. "I have a hard time keeping my two-year-old from eating dirt much less stepping in it."

It is a truism of politics in the U.S. today that many communities and many Americans like these—the people who have suffered at the blunt end of economic decline and who have been left behind—have been wooed by a new brand of right-wing politics fueled by that resentment. It is a brand that found its most potent voice, ironically, in a billionaire real estate developer from Queens.

There is plenty of that here as well. This attachment to Trumpism becomes even more evident as you move out beyond the city limits to the rural communities nearby. Here is where land is more open and families and homes are more distant from one another. Here is where the words "liberty" and "freedom" have deep resonance, expressed in the language of deer hunting, Harleys, and signs on the wall that show a menacing handgun and the words: WE DON'T DIAL 911.

Generations ago, working-class and rural families like those living here might have displayed a portrait of Franklin Roosevelt or John F. Kennedy on their walls. Now there are Trump flags flying over homes in a way that seems permanent. It is not by coincidence that the voters here in Niagara County supported Trump for president by wide margins. Today no local fair seems complete without a booth selling Trump merchandise (most of it manufactured in China). In our unexpected move to Lockport I would stumble into a political education that was not going to be theoretical or distant.

I found a community where people's roots run deep and where people have a deep history together. Most Lockportians (as they are called), even into their fifties and sixties, are still close friends with the people they sat together with at Lockport High School decades before. Graduating classes still hold regular reunion luncheons fifty years after they received their high school diplomas. Many people live in the same houses they have lived in since they were first married. It is not unusual to overhear a group of gray-haired women reminiscing about a sleepover they had together in the fifth grade.

One thing that all this familiarity of place and people translates into is an admirable amount of community solidarity. Volunteer organizations here are numerous. So are community fundraisers for people who have suffered an illness, a house fire, or some other calamity. It is a culture of solidarity that spreads regionwide. A winter ago during a massive blizzard, dedicated Buffalo Bills fans famously grabbed their snow plows to rescue the snowed-in players from their homes so they could get to a game. I tell people elsewhere that if you are ever in a natural disaster you want to be in Western New York. People have each other's backs and know how to do very practical things.

However, as Lockport's mayor, Michelle Roman, would tell me, all that familiarity and solidarity is a double-edged sword: "We have this backbone of, 'We are Lockport, we are Western New York, we support each other and we don't need any outsiders.' But then that also closes you off to a broader sense of the world." That leaves the door wide open for prejudice and fear of what is not familiar. Even small changes can provoke a major public response. Two of the loudest recent public uproars been over moving the Fourth of July fireworks show and converting a traffic light into a four-way stop. Bigger changes, like claims that immigrants might be relocated here, cause a bigger uproar still.

It is also clear that vibrant community identity does not also translate into vibrant local democracy. Lockport's local city elections rarely draw a voter turnout of more than one voter in four. Local school elections rarely draw more than one in ten. Citizens speaking out at local government meetings is such an unusual occurrence that it often lands on the front page of the newspaper. The issue that drew the most speakers recently was whether to allow the keeping of chickens within the city limits (approved). There seems to be an invisible line where concern for community crosses over into "Oh, you're making it political now." That lack of interest is an open invitation to shady players looking to raid the public purse.

The city's housing is a map of its development over many decades. Along Locust Street and Pine Street, not far from the city's center, you can find blocks of beautiful old mansions built in the Civil War era for the city's wealthiest. A few streets away you will find blocks of small houses built in the 1920s and 1930s for the workers at the Harrison Radiator factory. Some of these were ordered and delivered in pieces from Sears and Montgomery Ward catalogs then assembled on site. Outward from there are blocks of squat homes built in the 1960s and 1970s when GM expansions put the city to work. In the 1980s a flock of vinyl-sided colonials was built, filling in what remained of the city's largest plots of vacant land.

The city's driveways are a map of its current economics. On the more affluent streets the homes are accompanied by lookalike late-model hatchback SUVs, the vehicle of choice for moving around children and dogs.

There are also late-model pick-ups used to cart the materials needed for never-ending home improvement projects. The driveways of poorer neighborhoods are populated by aging sedans and trucks that are older, some with the winter signature of rusted-out fenders.

Great wealth and great poverty live here side by side. One of the wealthiest men in town, David Ulrich, lives in a mansion with gleaming white pillars in the style of a Greek temple. A ten-minute walk away live some of the most low-income families in Lockport, mostly in run-down rental units. The children of the poorest walk past the big white mansion on their way to the high school. In Lockport everyone is keenly aware, up close, of how all the other layers of the economic layer cake live.

Lockport is also a place divided deeply by race. It is a city with not a single Black police officer or firefighter, not a single Black member of the Common Council and not a single Black man teaching in a public school system in which more than 1 in 10 students are Black. It is a city where one more Black man, Troy Hodge, died in the hands of White police officers.

Against the backdrop of those complexities, Lockport remains a city wrapped in all the signs of small-town ritual. In the mornings and evenings people across town take their dogs out for walks. On trash days blue plastic bins are lined up at the curb like obedient sentries standing guard. Seven days a week Tom's Diner draws a steady crowd of people sitting across from one another in red vinyl booths. On Saturdays in summer local farmers and vendors gather for the weekly community market by the city's historic locks. Autumn is marked by the start of football practice at the high school. Holidays like St. Patrick's Day and the Fourth of July are celebrated with full enthusiasm. At Christmas, Santa returns to greet the local children in his tiny well-decorated cottage in a neighborhood park.

It was into that mix of history, conservatism, diversity, division, and scattered Americana that my family and I landed in the summer of 2017 for what we thought would be a short while. As it turned out, our short while became indefinite. It also turned out that I loved it here.

I loved Lockport's quiet simplicity, which is about all I could have handled after living in rural Bolivia for so many years. I loved that we were surrounded by farmland all the way out to Lake Ontario, that I could transport myself most anywhere I wanted to by bicycle, and that ample nature was rarely far away. What I loved most was that Elizabeth and Michael bought the house across the street from us and that we ended up living so close to our two granddaughters that we can yell to each other from our front porches. Life does not get better than that.

As we made the decision to stay I assumed that I had entered a new era of my life that would be quieter than the one we had just finished in Bolivia. I would be just another anonymous old guy with a short white beard, leaning into a new life as Gapa and as the father of a teenage daughter moving much too swiftly through high school and her last years under our family's roof. I assumed wrong.

Births

Our granddaughter, Isabella Rose Mulligan, was born just past 2 p.m. on a late August afternoon in 2017, a few weeks after our arrival in Lockport. At the local hospital the nurses were astounded by her full head of thick black hair. I told them, "You know what they call babies born in Bolivia who have a full head of thick black hair? They call them *every* baby."

Lynn and I had been at the hospital all the night before, so afterward I pedaled my bicycle across town to get a much-needed coffee. My vintage red bike was one of the few things of actual use that had emerged from the San Francisco storage unit we had ridiculously kept for the two decades we were out of the country.

En route I decided to stop off at the drug store and pick up a copy of that day's *Lockport Union-Sun & Journal*. I thought it would make a nice keepsake one day for the tiny girl who had just made me a grandfather. Inside on the paper's editorial page was an opinion column by Nicholas L. Waddy, a conservative history professor at a small nearby state college. His personal blog site featured photos of such personal heroes as Spiro Agnew and Margaret Thatcher, along with his self-description: "Political commentator, historian, patriot, novelist, and wise man extraordinaire!"

His column in the paper was titled, "Republicans: Stand with Trump on the Wall." It called on Republicans in Congress to shut down the U.S. government until Democrats agreed to include funds in the federal budget to build Trump's border wall with Mexico (the one Trump had promised that Mexico would pay for): "Republicans in Congress: America wants the wall. America, moreover, is going to get a wall. Trump will make sure of that, even if he has to build it himself. Get on board, therefore, stand with the president, and accept nothing less than a budget that protects America's borders fully and completely. Victory is at hand, so let us grasp it together." This is how I came to spend my first evening as a grandfather writing an opinion column for Lockport's daily newspaper and emailing it in for publication. It ran two days later under the headline: "Trump's Mexico Wall is Foolishness Run Amok." "President's Trump's wall, according to an MIT study, would cost as much as $40 billion to build (and more to maintain). To put that very large number in perspective, that is enough to cover the annual Social Security payments to half a million seniors, or pay for a year's worth of pre-school for 9 million children. Proponents of the wall, however, think it a higher priority to spend it on a 1,000-mile-wide mass of concrete." Looking back on it now, I can see all the ways in which my column was utterly tone deaf given the local audience. With its pile of statistics and smug self-assuredness I am sure it convinced no one of anything except perhaps that some strange new leftist had come to town. These were all lessons I would have to learn later.

The column was actually the second time I had appeared in the pages of the *Union-Sun & Journal*. Several years before we moved to Lockport I was in town for a visit with Elizabeth en route to have Thanksgiving with my family in California. It was my first time back in the U.S. for the holiday in almost two decades, and I was excited about it.

We were having lunch in Scripts Café, which occupies a ground-floor corner of the old restored Palace Theater. Escaping the late autumn cold outside, a young reporter for the paper came in looking for people to interview for a regular feature called, *What Your Neighbors Are Saying*. He came over to our table and we agreed to help him with his question of the day: What are you looking forward to most for Thanksgiving?

My intelligent daughter gave a short answer about food. "Pumpkin pie especially," she told him. I rambled that I was visiting from Bolivia and told him that I was looking forward to spending Thanksgiving with my family in the U.S. for the first time in twenty years. When the paper came out the next morning, Elizabeth's food reply was there, short and sweet. My answer had been edited down to, "I am looking forward to having Thanksgiving with my family for the first time in 20 years." Elizabeth laughed and told me, "It makes you sound like a total loser whose family wouldn't have Thanksgiving with him for twenty years." It would be the first of my Lockport lessons about writing—fewer words, and if they are about food, even better.

While my column on the Trump Wall certainly did not win over any converts, it did bring me together at Scripts Café once again the week after it was published with the newspaper's editor, Joyce Miles. A cheerful woman in her forties, Joyce was a twenty-five-year veteran of local journalism in the area. She began her career with the paper at a young age, working in the composing room where the news was still laid out with the aid of an exacto knife. From there she became a local beat reporter, an editor, and then the woman in charge of a newspaper that was founded four years before the Erie Canal was opened. Joyce was also a one-woman encyclopedia about all things Western New York.

By the time we had finished our coffees we had also cooked up a plan. I would write an opinion column for the newspaper two Wednesday mornings a month. The content was entirely up to me. It could be about national issues, global ones, or local ones. It could be hard edged or soft.

Some people do woodwork as a hobby, some golf, others paint. My new hobby would be to write an opinion column for the thirty-five hundred subscribers of the local daily newspaper. The birth of our granddaughter not only brought us to Lockport but had also unexpectedly turned me into a local writer and had given me an unexpected opportunity to learn about the political and cultural divide taking over the country.

My first official column ran in September, the day after I turned sixty. It was titled, "Morning Rituals on Two Sides of the World." It was a friendly piece that compared the rituals of mornings in two utterly different places, Bolivia and Lockport. I wrote about the challenge that I faced in both places getting our youngest daughter, Mariana, to school on time:

> Then come the obstacles I can't control. In Bolivia this might mean that our neighbor Fructoso has chosen the exact same moment to move his amazingly slow cows down our dirt and rock road. Or all the bus drivers in the city may decide to blockade the main streets to demand a fare increase. In Lockport the roads are reasonably paved and up to now I have encountered not a single herd of cows walking down Locust Street. The main obstacle seems to be a rather long traffic light at Lincoln Avenue.

Readers seemed to enjoy it. Weeks later I wrote a very different column, dipping into national politics and taking aim at President Trump's proposed giant federal tax cut. It was being sold as a plan for the middle class, but the serious money was going to corporations and the very wealthy. I used a long and flawed metaphor about a shady car salesman that sounded a lot like Trump:

> "Uhhh, that doesn't look like a real Tesla."
> "Oh, but it is! It's just sold under a different name—the Toyota Watt! But, really it's a Tesla."

"And this runs on electricity?"

"Are you kidding me? Electricity, gas, whatever you want! See the cord here? You can drive it off the lot today, right now. We charged it up for you last night."

In the drafting stage I showed the column to my son-in-law, Mike, my personal advisor on all things Lockport. I thought he'd think it was clever. Instead he told me simply, "Too many words."

He was right. It not only had too many words but just missed the mark entirely. People who loved Trump were never going to believe the con man narrative about him. Others just decided to overlook it. A lot of readers, I came to learn, just liked the idea of cutting taxes in general no matter who really benefited. My learning continued.

Lessons on Facebook

On the first day of October news arrived that a shooter packing an arsenal of weapons had opened fire on a packed country music festival in Las Vegas, killing sixty people. It was the latest in a series of mass shootings that included the Sandy Hook Elementary School in Connecticut and a nightclub in Florida, but the scale of the death in Las Vegas was even larger. I published a column titled, "A Nation Drowning in a Sea of Guns": "But there are lots of crazy and violent people in other countries too. The difference is that we don't hand them semi-automatic weapons capable of sending bullets into six-year-olds at the rate of 45 rounds per minute. When the Second Amendment was joined to the Constitution the common gun on hand was a flintlock musket." Afterward I tried an experiment. I posted the column on a local Facebook group called "Lockportians." The group has a huge membership, just shy of twenty thousand people, almost as many as Lockport has residents.

Popular topics in the group include recommendations for veterinarians, expressions of gratitude to people who paid for other people's orders in line at McDonald's, pictures of pets both lost and found, and complaints about potholes. My favorite posts involved a long-running debate about whether the local Tim Hortons was properly preparing its grilled cheese sandwiches (majority opinion suggested it was not).

The Lockportians group also had occasional political posts, mostly scattered memes lauding President Trump, or complaints that local officials weren't getting the streets plowed fast enough. Into that collage of local life

I tossed in my column about guns in America. It didn't take long to get a response. By the end of the day there were more than two hundred replies in the comments section. Most came from gun owners who were not happy:

> "Until you can get the guns out of the bad guys hands don't take ours."

> "Why make me vulnerable and empower the criminals. I have the right to defend myself in today's MOB culture."

Others insisted that the problem was not guns but mental health and the general moral decline of the nation:

> "It's not a gun problem. It's a mental health issue and the result of poor parenting not teaching respect for human life in general. I realized after the Viet Man [sic] war that there were countries, non Christian primarily, that do not respect the value of a human life. They believe in reincarnation, so it doesn't matter if someone dies, they will come back. Or there is no heaven or hell, so what the heck, you just die. You cannot change their morals."

> "It's the moral decay thru out [sic] America that is the prevalent reason for this slaughter of innocent people."

There were also comments, far fewer of them, from people who agreed new gun laws were needed:

> "I agree with you. I do not like guns at all. They're justified by saying they make people feel 'safe' but for me it's the complete opposite."

One reader invited me to join him at a local firing range to test out various weapons for myself. I respectfully declined the offer.

The issue of guns was one where I learned something listening to people whose views were a lot different than mine. I arrived in Lockport with a pretty standard position that we should just get rid of guns altogether if we could. Then I started hearing from people who told me that hunting is a revered tradition in their family, passed down generation to generation. Others told me different versions of, "I live in the countryside. If it's two in the morning and you hear an intruder in your house and you have two toddlers in the next room and you want to call 911 and hope for the best, that is your right. In my house we have a gun."

When I tell these things to friends in places like Brooklyn and Berkeley I'll hear back something like, "Don't they understand that statistics show that having a gun at home is more likely to put them at risk than to make them safer?" The gun owners I've met in Western New York aren't making choices based on data, and they don't want those choices taken away by other people.

On the issue of banning AR-15–style assault weapons, here I found openings among gun owners who know well the difference between those guns of war and a hunting rifle, and who support some restrictions. With others, though, it seemed like I was speaking through a broken translation device. No matter what I said it came out the other side as, "We are coming to take away every gun you own."

My education continued.

By posting my columns on the local Facebook group I was able to combine the old-school pages of a local daily newspaper and the newer platform of social media, reaching a much wider and more diverse audience and getting instant feedback. It became a powerful way to hear from people with a different point of view.

In the months that followed I wrote about a variety of national issues, including immigration and President Trump's efforts to deport the young people brought here illegally by their immigrant parents many years before, a group known as the "Dreamers." That column posted in Lockportians drew strong reaction and also some useful insight:

> "Then they need to stay here when they take the proper steps to become a citizen. Otherwise, time to create a new life back home. Nothing is free."

> "How many have applied for American citizenship in those 20 years during their TEMPORARY time here?"

> "Can't they return to their home country and apply for US citizenship?"

There were also responses to those comments that were more sympathetic:

> "They were brought by their parents or family. If they've stayed this long and assimilated into society just like any other person, why shouldn't there be a legal path?"

It is easy to dismiss every anti-immigrant sentiment in the US as simply another form of racism. And while there is certainly a lot of racism involved, there is also something else. Many of the people commenting did not understand that these young "Dreamers" did not already have a legal route to US citizenship. When I pointed that out, many readers said that they thought there should be a legal way for them to get that citizenship. I have heard the same in many conversations here, essentially: I don't have a problem with immigrants coming here, but it needs to be done legally.

I wrote several columns about global climate change and every time the comment floodgates on Facebook opened up, starting with a regular chorus of denial:

> "Climate will change no matter what you do it's been doing it for millions of years and it will continue to do it."

> "According to past articles the world was supposed to spin uncontrollably . . . and Florida should be under water by now !! The world was supposed to end about 1000 times already!! Give me a break !!"

Some went right for Christian fatalism:

> "I can tell you have never read the Bible mainly Revelations, we are experiencing end times. What I can tell you is that God is in charge and there is nothing man can do to change the outcome of what's happening in this world. It's really the best time to be ready for Christ's return."

Others raised legitimate practical concerns about the expansion of renewable energy:

> "Everyone hears the slogan "renewable energy" they think oh, clean energy, sun and wind . . . but never thinking about all the energy it takes to build them and all the nasty components in them. And then, what do we do with all the nasty components when they no longer work?"

And there were some, fewer, who expressed support for action:

> "Growing up in Lockport and now with grandkids, our winters are no where's near what they use to be when I was a kid. The changes are noticeable when you take the time to think back to when and realize it now."

> "Take away from these comments. 1. Science is scary. 2. Facebook does a great job spreading dis/misinformation 3. Lockport is full of climate change experts."

I would learn much more about local opinion on these issues when I dove later into the local battles over solar and wind projects, a story for a later chapter in this book.

Of all the topics I have written about, the one that always seems to provoke more reaction is when I write about Donald Trump, including a January 2018 column marking his first year in office, and raising questions about his overt racism (i.e., Mexicans are rapists), his blatant lies (three million illegal immigrant voters) and his putting corporate moguls in charge of regulating their industries (coal barons dismantling clean water rules). The responses I received were another lesson.

> "How can he be racists [sic] when more African-American votes [sic] for him than the last 2 Republican candidates, You can't claim something that's subjective as a lie. It is unprovable how many illegal aliens voted. You would be much more persuasive if you argued against his policy."

> "He is not a politician and so if you expected him to act and talk like a politician you are totally wrong in your expectations. The man doesn't care a bit if you are black or white or purple or brown. He doesn't care if you are male or female or undecided. He cares about green and once you can understand that, and only that will you begin to understand him."

The most vocal booster of Trump locally is a fellow named Doug Newman, who posts regularly. I found his full-throated defense of Trump to offer some useful insight into why people in places like this one are so drawn to him:

"Until Donald Trump was elected, no one had been elected president in our lifetime who had not first been vetted by the party elite of one party or another. They had made their deals and agreed to play ball and follow the rules of the game as it is played in Washington. They had 'waited their turn.' If you looked at what they did instead of what they said, there was very little to choose between them. President Trump is the first president in over 100 years to be elected by the people in spite of the political elite, not because of it. He can't be bought, and he won't be managed. He comes from a world where results are what count, not how many empty promises you can make. He puts America first whenever he makes a decision and doesn't sell the office for personal gain or position. I can deal with his shortcomings because he fights for me and what made this nation great. That's my President. God Bless President Trump and stay your course."

I did write one other column that wasn't about Donald Trump directly, but about a Trump flag flying over the house of a nearby neighbor, one that read, TRUMP 2024, FUCK YOUR FEELINGS! There was a lot of reaction to this column, from a few defenders but mostly from other neighbors:

"It's called freedom of speech, and is protected by the constitution of the united states. . . . If you don't like it go back to the country you come from."

"I think it's their right, but it does make them look like complete jerks to everyone else. Whatever they say, to most of us they just want attention and like being confrontational with no regard for their community."

"One thing to use that word in the privacy of your own home . . . But when you got it broadcasted where little kids, churchgoers, decent people who don't use that language got to read this hanging off a flagpole in your front yard. . . . Whoever did that should seriously seek counseling."

"When my ten year old asked why it said that I cried."

I never heard from my neighbor flying the flag, but I did notice a few weeks afterward that the Trump flag had been taken down. Again, my education continued.

Columns of Another Kind

As any good maker of compost understands, you need to mix together a combination of things in order to produce good soil. The same is true of my Lockport columns, so along with the political and the provocative I have been careful to mix in columns of a different kind. In one I interviewed our dog, Lola, about her move from Bolivia to Western New York:

> Jim: What would you say you like most so far about Lockport?
>
> Lola: Hands down, no question, the squirrels. Whoever invented those, absolute genius! Basically they are dog toys that don't require some human to toss them around. They have some kind of self-propulsion system inside I think. They just whip by all on their own, fast, across lawns, down sidewalks and even up trees. They run up those trees and then I have to just stare way up at them, for hours. Yeah, I really love squirrels.

I wrote about the wonderful weekly Lockport Community Market, which had just moved into a new winter home in the old downtown Harrison Radiator building.

> As soon as you push open the heavy metal door that leads to the Market's winter home, you know it is about a lot more than buying and selling. The first thing you walk past is a set-up of local musicians who have come to bring song to a gathering of neighbors. I met a local man selling flavored waffles who proudly explained that he was still using his grandmother's original recipes. You'll also find at least one member of the mother and daughter team of Margaret and Jeanna from Stone Hollow Farm in Middleport. I do my best to control my intake of their amazing scones—small butter explosions in every bite.

The market vendors clipped the column and circulated it. I began to see the way that a newspaper columnist could help glue a community together by writing about what we shared and loved.

In another column I wrote about the immigrant English class where Lynn and I had become volunteers, titled, "Singing Green Eggs and Ham with Lockport's Immigrants":

> Recently I drew on a lesson I learned as a volunteer before, helping small children learn new words—sing them. So I brought in one of my favorite books, *Green Eggs and Ham* by Dr. Seuss.
>
> Soon enough the whole room is singing together in a collection of thick accents:
> *I will not eat them on a boat! I will not eat them with a goat!*
> *I will not eat them here! I will not eat them there!*
>
> Lockport is fortunate to have these people among us. We can learn from them. They are strong and resilient people. But apparently, for some reason that remains a mystery, they do not like green eggs and ham."

I began a tradition of publishing an annual April Fool's Day column. In one, just after a giant supertanker had famously gotten stuck in the Suez Canal, I laid out an elaborate story of how Erie Canal workers had come up with the answer that successfully freed it, an elaborate scheme involving mules. Workers at the maintenance facility told me readers had come by to congratulate them. In the runup to the 2024 solar eclipse, which reached totality in Lockport and generated huge excitement, I published an elaborate column about NASA making a math error and the eclipse passing us by. I heard afterward from many people it had fooled.

I have written many columns about my family, from the joys of newly arrived babies to the bittersweet experience of dropping off my youngest daughter for her last day of high school. In one I wrote about becoming a grandfather:

> She had magical powers even while in my daughter's womb, drawing us to Lockport from far away and planting us here. Today we both like Cheerios, though to be honest a lot of hers fall into her bib when she eats. One year a grandfather, such a blessing. Enjoy them while you can my friends. The part of our life's road where the new ones and the old ones walk together

(or crawl) does not last long in the scheme of things, and it is a very sweet road.

Later I wrote a column about my weekly visits to read books to the children in her pre-kindergarten class:

> Last week we had a rousing reading of Curious George the Monkey. I even had a yellow hat to wear, so I literally was The Man in the Yellow Hat. There is a secret to reading aloud to a group of children and keeping them engaged. Try not to be a grown-up. Happily, this is not a big stretch for me. When I read Caps for Sale, we all become the monkeys in the trees shaking our fists and stomping our legs. When we read Everyone Poops, I ask them all if everyone in their family makes poop. Preschoolers love this.

These columns were fun to write and some of the most popular. They also taught me one more lesson: If you want people to read the political articles that they might disagree with, remind them from time to time that you are a human being just like them. And if you can, make them laugh.

Turning Attention to the Local

As a newcomer to Lockport, local issues weren't really anything I knew about or had planned to write about. But I began to dip my toe in the water, starting with a column calling out our local state senator, Rob Ortt, a Republican who has since become the minority leader of the New York Senate. It took aim at a deliberately misleading photo-op with the leaders of the Lockport School District:

> In the photo Mr. Ortt holds a giant check to the district in which his name—*Senator Robert Ortt*—is emblazoned in huge letters across the top, in the manner of a check made out from his personal account. It seemed an incredible act of personal generosity by a local politician. Well, except it wasn't. The check represented a $50,000 line item from the New York state budget. A more honest check would have had the words 'Taxpayers of Lockport' written across it as the generous donor.

In another column I called out the Niagara County clerk for inventing a fake crisis about illegal immigrants storming local voting booths:

> Last week the Niagara County Clerk, Mr. Joseph Jastrzemski, sent an official letter to the President of the United States in which he warned of a "conspiracy" against our democracy, one that he says, "will forever poison the election process in New York State." His warning is that undocumented immigrants are preparing to flood the ballot box [using the new state drivers licenses they had become able to obtain]. More than half the people who are actually citizens here can't even be bothered to vote. But Mr. Jastrzemski thinks that undocumented immigrants are going to risk deportation to cast a ballot. Seriously?

During the City of Lockport's mayoral election in 2019 I wrote a column about anonymous robocalls launched against Mayor Michelle Roman, a special education teacher and Democrat who had first won the mayorship the previous year in a special election:

> Starting on Tuesday voters all over Lockport began receiving mysterious 'robocalls' from an unidentified source. From the cowardice of anonymity someone was trying a last minute smear to try to push Mr. Wohleben [the Republican candidate] into office. Mr. Wohleben claims he has no idea at all who is behind them. That means one of two things—either Mr. Wohleben is lying or there is a secret group of very powerful and very slimy people working hard to put him in charge of our city.

Over time, calling out local political antics and hypocrisy became a staple of my columns. But I also wrote about slices of local life that deserved more attention.

I wrote about the old 1860s one-room schoolhouse and the wonderful young couple, Barbara and Chris Pease, who had lovingly renovated it into the Schoolhouse Wellness Center offering yoga classes, massage, and other healings. I published a column on the Lockport Nature Trail, with its ancient oak trees and its dedicated caretaker, a retired GM engineer named Kenneth Horvath. I wrote a piece called "Joy of Bagels" about Frank Rezarch who brought real New York bagels to Lockport's Main Street with his new shop, B&D bagels. I wrote about the new Lock City Bookstore and its special feature, a room where you can play with kittens up for adoption (my granddaughters call this "the kitty store"). In the summer of 2023 I published a series of columns under the title Positively Lockport, profiling some of my favorite local musicians, businesses, and more.

My column in the venerable *Union-Sun & Journal* ended up becoming all kinds of things at once—a place to test out ways to talk about national issues, a tool for holding local politicians to account, and a way to express gratitude to the people I was meeting here who were dedicating themselves to their community in so many creative ways. It became my own way to contribute as well.

"Are You the Writer?"

The first time it happened Lynn and I were out at a local bar and restaurant, Lock 34, named for one of the Erie Canal locks. It was midwinter in Lockport and eating out like this was one of the few occasions when the people around us became something more recognizable than just bundled-up figures in thick parkas walking their demanding dogs through the snow.

As we sat at our table, a woman who I did not know had just put on her coat and was heading out the door. As she passed us she quietly stopped and said to me in a hushed voice, "I love your columns." Then she disappeared. It was as if she was sharing a secret she felt was better kept quiet. I turned to Lynn, "Well, that was something."

It happened again a few weeks later when I was in the checkout line at a local Walgreens. The young man working the register eyed me a little longer than what one would expect and then asked, "Are you that guy who writes for the newspaper?" I suppose it wasn't that hard to figure out, since my column always ran with my picture.

"I don't agree much with your politics, but I do think you were right in that article about the schools," he said as he cashed me out. I thanked him and began to think that maybe there was actually something going on here. As our first spring came and people began to be out and about more, encounters like these became more frequent. One Sunday morning as I sat with a coffee in a friend's store, an older fellow approached me and said, "I'm a Republican and I don't agree with you on many issues, but I respect that you are actually offering up reasoned thought and not just ranting."

The frequency of encounters like this increased. As I walked Lola in a local nature trail one evening, a gentleman recognized me and wanted to talk about something I'd written about solar power. In the Saturday market one weekend several people wanted to talk about a series I'd recently published on race in Lockport. This began to happen over and over again: during a local garden tour, at the playground with my granddaughters, in line at the produce store, and more.

One night my son-in-law, Mike, and I met up for some beers at a local pub near my house. Sitting at the bar next to us was a middle-aged couple who looked like they were out for an evening and were clearly several rounds of drinks ahead of us. The woman looked at me in a way that was beginning to feel familiar, only with a little more blur. "Hey, are you that writer?" I told them that I was and we had a good, though slightly inebriated, conversation about some recent things I'd written about.

The other thing that made me noticeable to people is my bicycle. I pretty much do all my local travel on my old red bicycle, even through parts of the winter. Unlike in a car, on a bike you can actually interact with people as you pass by. Sometimes as I am riding I'll notice a car approaching from behind me and then slowing as it gets close. As I turn to the side to look, I'll see a window open, and the driver inside will say something to me like, "I like your columns." Then the window closes up again, and we both go our separate ways. This has happened many times now. People here may not always agree with my point of view, but they do seem grateful that I am writing about our community in a way that feels straightforward and honest.

Later when I ended up in a long and very public battle with the Lockport School District (I'll get to that in the next chapter) a reporter for the paper, Connor Hoffman, had a meeting with the district superintendent and her assistants. He came back with an interesting piece of news. "They never refer to you by name," he told me. "They refer to you only as 'the writer.'" That gave me an idea. I changed the name of my column to "The Writer" and publicly thanked the superintendent and district staff for the suggestion.

As I waded into my sixties I did not think of myself as a writer. Writing has always been an adjunct to the thing I actually did. As a young legislative assistant I learned to write memos that condensed complex state policy down to what a distracted politician could absorb at a glance. As an advocate I wrote op-ed articles aimed to make people care about something in 750 words or less. I did also write four books, on US politics, Bolivian revolution, and other topics. But all these were still by-products of my actual work at the time.

Here in Lockport, oddly, I became the town writer. That is different than being a journalist. We have news reporters here, good ones. But their job is to cover the day-to-day developments in our community, not the wider picture. That is what I do now. I tell stories that lift up the larger meaning of things that often get missed in daily reporting.

There are four stories in particular that I have had the opportunity to write in depth on local issues with national ramifications. One is about how fears over school safety led the Lockport School District to waste millions of dollars to become the first district in the country to deploy facial recognition surveillance in its hallways. Another is about what it means to be Black in a White, conservative community. A third is the story about a rural rebellion against renewable energy and its implications for the country's ambitious plans for clean energy. The last is a grand tale of old-school political corruption in a publicly owned gambling empire and the curse of local kleptocracy.

Chapter Two

Spy Cameras in the Schools

During our first frigid February here in 2018, the *Union-Sun & Journal* ran a brief story about an action taken by the Lockport Board of Education that seemed quite odd. It had approved a plan to install high-tech facial recognition surveillance cameras on school campuses across the district. The article reported: "Superintendent Michelle Bradley said Lockport schools already have surveillance systems in place. But the resolution would allow for the use of a new facial and shape recognition software provided by SNTech. Bradley called the SNTech software "above and beyond" other kinds of software. The project is estimated to cost around $3.9 million, which would be covered by the $4.2 million the district was given from the state's Smart Schools Bond Act, which New York voters approved in 2014." The reported cost (which later turned out to be $2.7 million) was enormous for a school district with fewer than 4,300 students. The use of technology deployed by authoritarian governments to spy on dissidents also seemed a strange approach to school security in a small city in Western New York.

Our youngest daughter, Mariana, was in her freshman year at Lockport High School at the time, and school safety was certainly something I cared about as a parent. The idea, however, of spy cameras in the schools seemed worth a deeper look. To be honest, there also isn't much to do in midwinter in Lockport, so I used my time to do some research. What I discovered was troubling.

In 2014 the voters of New York state approved something called the Smart Schools Bond Act. It allocated $2 billion of taxpayer funding to invest in new technology in the state's public schools. The focus was on updated laptops and iPads and faster internet connections, the kinds of things that would give students more opportunity to take full advantage of what technology in schools had to offer. Each district was allocated a share based on its number of students.

Lockport's share was $4.2 million, a fortune for a small district and one of the largest state grants it would ever receive. The district needed to submit a plan and supporting research for how it would spend the money and then get approval from state education officials.

At the same time, just across the Canadian border, a tiny two-man company working out of a small house in Gananoque, Ontario (population 5,200), was watching this and spotted what seemed like a golden business opportunity. At the end of the list of projects that could receive funding from the Smart Schools money, after new laptops and high-speed broadband, sat one more type of allowed purchase: "high-tech security."

The company, SNTech, was founded by Cameron Uhren and KC Flynn, two men who built their careers in neither education nor school security. They worked in Ontario's casino and gambling industry. Uhren, the CEO, had worked previously for the Ontario Lottery and Gaming Corporation. A Canadian state official at the time had denounced the agency for its "culture of scandalous spending." This included Uhren billing taxpayers $1,151.04 for a new suit to wear to a meeting.[1]

SNTech had previously developed a surveillance camera system that kept an eye on casino card tables and could catch signs of cheating dealers. Amidst increasing public concern over school shootings, the two men decided to market themselves as something else. They rebranded themselves as experts in how to deploy facial recognition surveillance systems as a school security measure. The company made no secret of who it targeted as its main market. It announced on its website: "Many State Governments have set aside funding for individual schools to use technology for a safer school environment. We are focused initially on the state of New York which has 14,800 public schools."

If the two men could get New York school districts to see their prototype system as a quick, high-tech fix to worries over school security—and with state money to pick up the tab—there was a fortune to be made. But no public school district anywhere in the country had ever installed a system like this inside a school. SNTech had never installed its system in any school anywhere nor did it have any track record to prove that their system actually worked.

What the tiny company needed, badly, was a school district somewhere willing to be their first buyer, one they could then cite as an example to convince others. Welcome to Lockport, New York.

A Salesman Comes to Town, in Disguise

Anthony Olivo (Tony, as he is known) is a large and muscular former US marshal and Cheyanne, Wyoming police officer, with an ample head as bald as an egg. After leaving his formal career in law enforcement he set up shop as a "criminal investigator" mostly helping corporations to root out fraudulent insurance claims. After the horrific massacre of twenty children and six adults at Sandy Hook Elementary school in 2012, Olivo tried to set himself up as something else: a school security expert.

Olivo began approaching local school districts in Western New York, including Lockport, and offered them a gift. He would conduct security assessments of their schools "for free." Officials in the Lockport district liked the price and accepted his offer.

At first Olivo's suggestions were relatively minor and standard, like redesigning school entrances so that visitors had to be buzzed in. But in 2015, after the New York Smart Schools Bond was passed, Olivo came back to Lockport with a new proposal. He suggested that the district spend $2.7 million of its state Smart Schools funds—two-thirds of all the money it would receive—to become the first public school district in the nation to install a facial recognition surveillance system inside its schools.

Introducing Olivo at a school board meeting in March 2018, the district's assistant superintendent for finance and management services, Deborah Coder, explained, "Tony is our security consultant. He does not charge us anything for giving us advice." At that same meeting the board's president also parroted the same tale of free advice. "There ha[ve] been some questions about Mr. Olivo's involvement in this project and what he gets out of it. We did not reach out to him. He reached out to us and provided free consultation to this district."

It would later turn out that Olivo's free advice was akin to the free advice you get from a salesman on a car lot. They only make the commission if they make the sale. According to school district documents obtained later by the New York Civil Liberties Union (NYCLU), behind closed doors Olivo and those same school district officials were negotiating a software licensing agreement that would pay more than $475,000 to Olivo's firm. The "security consultant" and SNTech were actually financial partners. Olivo was knocking on school district doors as a salesman.

As one legitimate school safety expert would explain to me later, the basics of evaluating school security are not rocket science. You hire an expert with no financial stake of any kind in any specific solution. You ask that expert to look at potential dangers and then draw up a list of options along with their pros and cons. By contrast, officials in the Lockport district put student safety and the district's budget into the hands of a man hawking an expensive and untested product.

The complicated pieces of all this were still falling into place, but after a week of digging around I knew there was a much bigger story going on than the district's happy talk about "above and beyond," so I decided to write about it in my column in the *Union-Sun & Journal*. I wasn't too sure how the editor there, Joyce Miles, would react to the idea of using my column to go after the local school district for what seemed like a clear scandal of incompetence and perhaps worse. Would this wander into sensitive local politics in a way she had not quite envisioned when she offered a strange newcomer a regular column just a few months earlier?

"Shit!" came her voice out of the receiver on my iPhone when I called her. "We should have broken this as a news story. Oh well, this will be new. We will break a story on the opinion page." She supported my work and the newspaper's reporting work on the facial recognition story from the start and would remain a fierce supporter of that digging for more than four years as the story continued to unfold.

On February 21, 2018, I ran a column under the title, "Lockport Schools' Security Plan Warrants Scrutiny." I acknowledged the worry many parents had about their children's safety in school and then explained the glaring foolishness in the district's plan. The school district would have to guess in advance who a school shooter would be, get his photograph, and put it in a database. Then the shooter would have to pass by one of the cameras and not be wearing a mask (ironically, not long afterward everyone coming and going from the school would be wearing a mask). Absent all of that, the $2.7 million system would do nothing at all. I also explained the difference between these new high-tech cameras and the kind parents and students were used to having in schools: "You don't need facial recognition to monitor a hallway to see if a student is getting bullied, or to see who robbed a student locker. Regular cameras can do that. Facial recognition systems are designed to look for specific people. Some airports use them to look for suspected terrorists. The Russian government uses them to monitor the movement of dissidents it doesn't like. But what does that accomplish in a public school?" My column pointed out how neighboring districts spent their Smart Schools monies on practical things like new computers and iPads and called out the school district for its total lack of consultation with the community before buying the system. The only evidence of any community consultation at all involved a public comment session held during a school board meeting in August 2016, which not a single member of the public attended. Even the president of the teacher's union told the newspaper that the project had been a surprise to him as well.

If you are a school district that wants to pretend to be serious about public input but doesn't actually want input or scrutiny, there is no better way to do that than by scheduling it for a midweek afternoon in August. Nonetheless, in their application for state funding, district officials certified that they had consulted with parents, students, teachers, and members of the community, as the state required. It was a lie.

At this point reporting on the story by the news staff at the paper kicked into full gear as well, asking new questions of district officials, who bristled at every new effort at scrutiny. Who would the system actually be programmed to look for? The district wouldn't say. How much was SNTech going to get for selling the system to the district? How much was Olivo going to get? Again, no answers. Exactly what technology was SNTech offering the district? That information was proprietary and secret, said the company. With every answer the scent of a very bad deal only grew stronger.

A Time Machine Back to the 1950s

My visit to the meeting of the Lockport Board of Education in late March 2018 felt like a trip back in time to somewhere in the late 1950s.

The members of the board sat along a set of long wooden tables at the front of the meeting room, facing two rows of chairs on the opposite side set aside for visitors. I soon learned that Lockport Board of Education meetings don't get many visitors. In between was a camera and microphone set up by the local public access television station, which broadcasts the meetings live for anyone at home who might think it was a good way to spend a Wednesday evening.

For that particular meeting a new feature had been added to the mix, a pair of plainclothes security guards. I learned later from the young reporter for the newspaper that the guards had been added just for me and my public announcement that I was going to the meeting to speak about the camera system.

In the good tradition of small-town culture, the meeting was brought to order with the recitation of the Pledge of Allegiance for which we were all invited to stand and place our hands over our hearts. After that, in honor of Technology Week, a pair of sneakered sixth-grade girls from Emmet Belknap Intermediate School offered a demonstration of a remote-controlled car they had programmed to knock over a set of cardboard toilet paper tubes on command.

The president of the Board of Education at that time was a gentleman named John Linderman, a thin, sour-faced fellow who worked as a county bureaucrat. At that time Linderman had already served on the board for five years longer than it takes to turn a kindergartner into a graduating senior. It was clear immediately that he considered the Board to be his fiefdom and one he kept under tight and formal control. He wielded a proper wooden gavel, which he used to tap the meeting briskly from item to item, referring always to the other members as Trustee (last name).

The school district's superintendent was Michelle Bradley, a woman in her fifties who was at the pinnacle of a three-decade career in the Lockport district. Bradley had risen through the district's ranks from fourth-grade teacher to the $200,000 per year post of district superintendent.

Even though it is a rare thing for a member of the community to come and speak at a board of education meeting in Lockport, the board had very clear protocols for such an event. People with something to say about an item on the meeting agenda were given a three-minute time slot to address the board at the start of the meeting. In a long explanation of the rules beforehand that took almost that same three minutes to recite, members of the public were informed that the board was under no legal obligation to hear from the public and did so as a courtesy only.

During my allotted 180 seconds I went through the same questions and criticism laid out in my columns. Where was the analysis that demonstrated that this $2.7 million system would do anything real to protect our children? Why was the district following the advice of a salesman instead of a bona fide school security expert? Had the district looked at all at the implications for student privacy under a system deployed at no other school in the nation?

The board members and district staff sat grim faced and silent for the duration. Not responding to any parents and taxpayers who show up to speak is also a strict part of the board's strange protocols.

The meeting began nearly an hour late. Beforehand the board and district staff had huddled in a long, closed executive session with Tony Olivo and the other contractors in line to get a piece of that $2.7 million, preparing for the presentation they would use to respond to the growing criticism of their facial recognition plans. The *Union-Sun & Journal* had run its own editorial that raised questions about the plan and called for a pause in the signing of any contracts until those questions were properly answered.

After a district PowerPoint presentation about the plan, Mr. Linderman acknowledged the recent coverage of the issue in the local newspaper and explained with a clear undertone of annoyance, "This project has been two years in the making and we have spent a considerable time on it."

Olivo smoothly repeated his story about approaching school districts after the Sandy Hook massacre to offer his guidance for free. He explained that he became aware of the facial recognition technology at an antiterrorism conference in 2015 and decided it would be a perfect fit for public schools.

He told the board and its small audience, "I know it may seem that this technology is brand new, but it's not. It's in use all over Europe. This technology is used by Interpol, Scotland Yard, the French Ministry of Defense, the Palace of Monaco." This was likely the same pitch he had used to convince district officials that this was what our schools needed as well. What was good for combating terrorism in Monaco was certainly the ideal way to protect students in Lockport.

Members of the board were largely cheerleaders for the project during the meeting, effusive over its capabilities. They also happily pointed out that it would be paid for entirely with a state grant rather than local tax funds, as if one pot of the public's money was all that different than another.

The one exception to this ebullient support was the board's lone Black member and its youngest, Victoria Obat (who would soon leave the board to attend law school). Only she was willing to ask Olivo point blank about charges that he had a conflict of interest. He responded simply with a lie, "I don't have a financial interest in this company. I don't." He said this despite the nearly half-million-dollar licensing agreement that Coder and Olivo had been negotiating in secret.

When the presentations were over, without further debate, the board of education voted 8–0 to approve the contract to purchase the system. Even Ms. Obat voted for the project. As I would learn from other board members later, behind closed doors our small-town board of education operated heavily on peer pressure. Executive sessions were not really discussions about protected topics like personnel matters. They were often bullying sessions, I was told, designed to keep errant board members in line.

Here was one other lesson about small-town life in Lockport. A local school district could be largely taken over by a small group of friends, who would hold power for many years and be shielded by a blanket of general public apathy. If a subject was of any serious importance they dived into an executive session behind closed doors. They became accustomed to being asked no questions. More than a few also found ways to put members of their family on district payroll. In Mr. Linderman's case this included, at different points, both his wife and two sons.

After the vote I ran into the district's director of assessment & technology, Robert LiPuma, in the reception area just outside the meeting room. LiPuma had been a key actor in the district's decision to buy the SNTech system. I had never met him before.

"Hi Rob, I just want you to know that there is nothing personal about this."

"Yeah, but what you are saying in the paper isn't true." He was agitated. He held a small stack of my articles in his hand, marked up in red ink.

"Ok, what specifically have I written that is factually inaccurate?" I asked.

"Here," he pointed to one of the marked-up columns. "You called the system 'experimental.' That's what they told me when I encouraged the district to buy iPads. They called those experimental too and now everyone has them."

I pondered this for a moment and replied, "Well, actually an iPad was really just a big iPhone, and lots of people already had those. But you guys are going to be the first district in the country to have these facial recognition cameras. That seems pretty experimental to me." I could see we weren't going to find much room for agreement. It also reinforced how flimsy the district's thinking actually was, despite the huge expense.

The next day's *Union-Sun & Journal* ran a story about the board meeting on the front page, summarizing the board's debate for what it was, and homing in on the question of Tony Olivo and his financial connection to the company selling the system. "Asked by the US&J about his consulting terms, Olivo declined to explain how he is paid by SNTech."

The reporter covering the story (and who would continue to dive into it ever more deeply for the next two years) was a twenty-three-year-old named Connor Hoffman. Rail thin with a brown scruffy beard that matched his hair, the Lockport School District was one regular "beat" among many for him at a newspaper with just two reporters on staff. A graduate of a local state university, SUNY Fredonia, Connor was still in his first year at the *Union-Sun & Journal* when he began covering "the cameras story" as it became known locally. I don't think there was any story he loved covering more. Spending Wednesday evenings sitting through dull Board of Education meetings was probably not what he had dreamed about as journalism student. But Lockport's high-tech surveillance experiment was on its way to becoming a national story, and he was on the front lines of it.

In a profile on Connor later, after the cameras story had drawn national interest, he explained to an interviewer: "You're young and right out of college and people don't take you seriously. That was in part what really made me hungry for the facial recognition story. I wanted to find something that needed to be investigated thoroughly and prove myself as a journalist."

Here was yet one more local lesson with much larger meaning. While thousands of small communities around the country were being thrust into news deserts as their daily and weekly papers closed down, Lockport still had a smart, fierce young reporter who dug into the details and an editor eager to keep his reporting on the front page. In other communities, a story like this one might well have received no public scrutiny at all.

The Public Reacts

As with other columns I had written for the newspaper, I posted my writing about the district's surveillance plan to the Lockportians Facebook group. Those posts, from the start, became an instant source of feedback about how people looked at the issue. In the beginning there were people who insisted that where school safety was concerned, any expense was worth trying:

"If it saves one child or teacher I am for it!"

"Small price to pay to keep my daughter safe."

This tendency of many people to declare "safety at all costs" had echoes in other debates nationwide over issues like police funding and spending on national defense. It shielded issues like those from hard questioning and often sidelined the questioners as being insufficiently committed to keeping people safe.

There were others, however, of every political stripe (by this time I knew who a lot of the vocal Trump supporters were) who saw through the foolishness of the plan and how it wasted taxpayer money that was supposed to benefit students:

> "Okay, so why do they think that would give more protection? It seems like metal detectors would make more sense."

> "I'm okay with using some of the money towards the improved Security. But agree that Facial Recognition is both unproven and questionably illegal and definitely a privacy concern. Don't like the fact that they said they consulted teachers and students but yet the Union said they weren't included in the discussions."

> "To put this system in at the expense of classroom technology is just a gut reaction to an emotional situation. It is not thought out at all as far as I am concerned."

> "I do care that they want our children safe but it feels like they got hustled by the monorail salesman in the Simpsons."

Over time I learned what parts of the cameras story resonated most with people here—what seemed convincing and what did not. In other parts of the country that might have been the privacy issue. This did spark some local concern, including by vocal conservatives who saw it as an extension of more government Big Brother intrusion. But that was not the part of the story that really struck a public nerve here. What did was the tale of wasted funds and the shady dealings of Tony Olivo and SNTech.

The right words to capture all this came from Deanna Mesi, the woman who cuts my hair. Deanna is a Lockport native and a graduate of the high school herself some twenty-five years before. She considered herself part of the community and regularly worked the polling station during local elections. Five days a week the men and women of Lockport would sit in her chair and speak their minds about everything from potholes to politics. She told me that more than a few of them had mentioned "those crazy cameras" that they'd read about in the paper.

"They didn't do their homework!" she told me one morning as she gave me a trim. There it was, the hook that cut through all the complexity and detail. The Lockport School District had blown $2.7 million because it had failed to do the very thing teachers tell their students from day one: do your homework.

I learned about local reaction to the cameras story, not just in Facebook comments, but as people approached me about it in person as I roamed around town. One afternoon that summer Lynn and I bicycled around the city to take in the annual gardens tour, "Lockport in Bloom." It is a glorious event in which dozens of talented backyard gardeners open up their yards for a weekend to anyone who wants to come by and have a look. At one garden we ran into a man my age who I had never met. Under a sprawling maple tree he asked if I was Jim Shultz who wrote for the paper. I said that I was, and he began to repeat back to me all the basic facts of the cameras story—the cost figures, the name of the security consultant, and more—shaking his head in disbelief at the district's foolishness.

Here was another lesson. Through a combination of clarity and repetition it was possible to create a community story that people would remember and absorb. That came to people in two ways. One was the ongoing news coverage of emerging details that Connor wrote for the front page. The other was my writings on the opinion page that would update the overall narrative that put those developments and details in context. It was a good combination, but the question was still whether it would change anything.

In the immediate aftermath of the school district's approval of the cameras contract I discovered a novel feature of school district governance in New York state. Under state law, districts have to submit their annual budgets for voter approval. These elections took place each year in May, on the same day as the annual school board election. I used my column in the *Union-Sun & Journal* to encourage voters to oppose the district's new budget unless school officials agreed to put the brakes on the facial recognition project. It ran under the headline: VOTE 'NO' ON SPY CAMERAS IN LOCKPORT'S SCHOOLS.

At this point the facial recognition system had become a major issue in the city. A father who was running for school board in that same election, Kyle Lambalzer, told me that as he walked door-to-door campaigning that the main issue people brought up was "the cameras." I had no illusion that this would change the outcome of the budget vote, but it seemed like one more way to keep the story in front of the public.

Old hands of local school politics, however, soon warned me that district officials had a ready response whenever anyone grumbled about approving school budgets. They would threaten an avalanche of bad things, from the cancelation of school buses to an end to school sports programs. Sure enough, district officials did exactly that, cleverly, in a response column from the coach of the Lockport High School football team, Joseph

Scapelliti. His column was titled, "Voting Down LCSD Budget Won't Stop Security Project." He wrote: "The actual impact of a 'NO' vote on the budget could be a drastic reduction in programs that benefit all students of Lockport City School District. These include but are not limited to music and art programming at all levels, athletics, full-day kindergarten, elementary libraries and district transportation services." In the end the budget passed, but by a much narrower margin than usual. The cameras controversy also propelled one of its critics, Mr. Lambalzer, to a first-place finish, defeating an incumbent who had been the system's chief booster on the board. In Lockport, the facial recognition system had been cemented as a political boondoggle by those in charge. But the real power of all this small-town noise was that it was about to break through the clouds to a much higher level.

Lockport's Spy Cameras Become a National Issue

School security was not solely a Lockport issue, it was a national one. Public concern and advocacy for proposed solutions were all on the rise in response to school shootings around the country. Parents, students, communities, educators, and lawmakers were all scrambling to find a way forward, and those ways were very different.

Political progressives were using public concern over school attacks to campaign for gun safety laws, especially aimed at weapons like the AR-15 and other assault weapons that played such a central role in the student massacres at Sandy Hook Elementary School in Connecticut, at Marjory Stoneman Douglas High School in Florida, and elsewhere. Political conservatives defended the mass ownership of military assault weapons and spoke instead of "hardening schools" with metal detectors and armed guards. In Lockport we had seen a preview of something else coming to world of school safety: profiteers pitching new forms of student surveillance as a high-tech answer.

If the Lockport School District was going to be insistent about blowing $2.7 million to be a high-tech guinea pig, then it could also serve as a national cautionary tale as well. The first step was to reach out to reporters beyond the boundaries of Lockport who might find the story worth their attention.

This began with the *Buffalo News*. The reporter who covered the small towns along the Erie Canal was Thomas Prohaska. He didn't need much prompting to see the newsworthiness of the cameras story, and his first article ran in mid-April of 2018 under the headline, LOCKPORT SCHOOLS TURN TO STATE-OF-THE-ART TECHNOLOGY TO BEEF UP SECURITY.[2] The article looked at the debate over how facial recognition technology misidentifies people of color and how the system could be used to track the movements of students and teachers. It also zeroed in on the conflict of interest of the "security expert" who had brought the system to the school district, Tony Olivo. Both he and Superintendent Bradley repeated the same misrepresentations that would later be contradicted directly in district documents: "'We don't get commissions. We don't own any part of SNTech. We have no financial interest in SNTech,' Olivo said. 'We haven't paid him one penny for this,' Bradley said." This would not be the last of the blatant public misrepresentations that would come back to haunt them both.

The real effect of the *Buffalo News* story, however, was that it acted like a bright red flare shot up into the sky. It helped spread the story to reporters who did not track what made news on the front pages of small papers like the *Lockport Union-Sun & Journal* but did pay attention to what got covered in larger regional papers like the *Buffalo News.*

Soon afterward I received an email from Drew Harwell, the lead technology writer at the *Washington Post*. He had read the *Buffalo News* article (in which I was quoted) and reached out for help with his own piece that ran in early June, "Unproven Facial-Recognition Companies Target Schools, Promising an End to Shootings."[3] "Although facial recognition remains unproven as a deterrent to school shootings, the specter of classroom violence and companies' intensifying marketing to local education officials could cement the more than 130,000 public and private schools nationwide as one of America's premier testing grounds—both for the technology's abilities and for public acceptance of a new generation of mass surveillance." I was quoted in the story as saying, "It is as if someone presented them with a cool new car and they didn't look under the hood."

The *Washington Post* article firmly established the Lockport cameras as a serious national story, Over the next few months, as the Lockport district and SNTech made preparations to install the new surveillance system, reporters from news outlets all over the country were reaching out for help with their own coverage: NPR, *Vice*, *Buzzfeed*, *Forbes Magazine*, and others. All these stories reported on high-tech surveillance in schools as a dubious proposition with a lot of unanswered questions.

Even MTV News got in touch. They were looking for a good hook for a young audience and settled on the idea of doing their feature on Connor Hoffman, the young journalist using old-school reporting to stay on top of a local story with national implications. Their video report in early 2020 also featured an interview with a group of Lockport High School students, including our daughter Mariana. The students told the MTV interviewers that they had never been informed about the system being set up to watch over them, or how it could be used to track their movements.

In the spring of 2019 the Lockport story finally landed in the *New York Times*. The paper had begun a new initiative called "The Privacy Project" to examine the implications of invasive technology. I suggested to the editors that they look into facial recognition surveillance in schools. They suggested back that I write an opinion article for the paper. My column, in June of that year, was titled "Spying on Children Won't Keep Them Safe" and reached a substantial national and global audience. I wrote:

> I have a 16-year-old daughter, and like every parent in the United States today, I worry about her safety when she's in school. But here in Western New York's Lockport City School District, those fears have led to a wasteful and dangerous experiment.
>
> The technology's potential is chilling. It would have the capacity to go back and create a map of the movements and associations of any student or teacher the district might choose. It can tell them who has been seen with whom, where and how often. District officials pledge that they would never deploy the software in that way, but if we have learned anything from the privacy breaches at Facebook and elsewhere, what matters is not what those in charge promise but what an intrusive technology has the capacity to do.

Six months later, at the start of 2020, the *New York Times* returned to the Lockport cameras story once again, this time dispatching one of its lead technology writers, Davy Alba, to travel here in midwinter and report the story herself. She spent two full days in Lockport, quizzing district officials with hard questions and interviewing everyone from students to the city's chief of police. Her article ran on February 6, 2020, on the front page of the newspaper's business section, "Facial Recognition Moves into a New Front: Schools." It's accompanying photographs included Lockport High School under a blanket of ice, and me, arms crossed and looking determined.

The *Times* article outlined the mechanics of the system and how Lockport came to acquire it. It included a good analysis of the technology's racial bias and its tendency to deliver false alarms. Olivo and SNTech had boasted that their system could also spot guns. Later we would learn that the system spat out so many false gun alerts (mistaking broom handles for rifles) that at one point the company advised the district to ignore the alerts altogether.

The police chief warned that any alert triggered by the system "would be treated as a live situation." This meant sending a pack of armed officers into the school looking for someone with a gun. A recent Lockport High School graduate, Jayde McDonald, connected the dots in the *Times* piece with a chilling warning. "Since the percentages for the false matches are so high, this can lead to very dangerous and completely avoidable situations." All it would take is one student pulling out a phone to take a photo and we could have had a huge case of needless tragedy. I told Alba that the school district had "turned our kids into lab rats in a high-tech experiment."

At this point Lockport's cameras had become the centerpiece of a genuine, full blown national debate.

The other outreach I did in the midst of all this was to legal and civil rights groups that had similar concerns about the privacy implications of high-tech surveillance. This included the New York Civil Liberties Union (NYCLU).

NYCLU's initial response was that the issue was interesting but that they were already too overstretched to take on anything new. Then after a series of staffing changes, a new lawyer came to the education team, Stefanie Coyle. She had begun her professional life as a kindergarten teacher and saw the urgency of the Lockport fight right away. She and NYCLU became smart and ferocious allies.

Stefanie and NYCLU began their work on the issue with a letter calling on New York Department of Education Officials to review their authorization of the Lockport project and to freeze any future approvals anywhere in the state. NYCLU's executive director, Donna Lieberman, said in a release to the news media: "Schools should be safe places for students to learn, not spaces where they are constantly surveilled. Lockport is sending the message that it views students as potential criminals who must have their faces scanned wherever they go." Then NYCLU sent the Lockport district a long list of undisclosed documents (nearly two dozen of them) that it was requesting under the New York Freedom of Information Law (FOIL). This included everything from the analysis that had been the basis of the district's decision to any records covering the financial relationship between the school district, SNTech, and Tony Olivo.

The State Education Department, which had approved the grant for the project with remarkably little scrutiny, responded by calling on the Lockport district to develop a privacy policy to govern the system's use. It also suddenly became noncommittal about whether Lockport still had state permission to turn the system on when it was ready.

While I was very grateful to have NYCLU's substantial state-level political weight and smart legal analysis on our side, I was also nervous about how a liberal advocacy group based in New York City would play with people in conservative Lockport.

In May 2019, the school district announced that it would begin testing the new system at the schools. Soon after, state education authorities gave their approval to the district to move forward based on its new privacy policy. The policy prohibited putting students' photos in the database of faces the system would look for but ignored the fact that the system would still record the faces and movements of every student anyway.

As Lockport's students returned from Christmas break in January 2020 the district quietly announced that the system had gone live: new cameras, secret database, unclear privacy policy, and all. I responded with a new column in the *US&J*, "The $2.7 Million Bonfire on Beattie Avenue": "How would we feel, as parents and as taxpayers, if the leaders of the Lockport school district went to the bank one afternoon, withdrew $2.7 million of district education funds in cash, took those giant bags of $100 bills and burned them in a bonfire in the district office parking lot? This now is the practical effect of the district's foolish facial recognition surveillance system, which officially went live last week after a year and a half delay."

Having the system go live at the start of 2020 accelerated the plans of Stefanie and other NYCLU staff to come to Lockport and meet with people in the community. We agreed to put together a public forum in late February at the Lockport Public Library. As it turned out the forum landed on the exact day that our eldest daughter, Elizabeth, gave birth to our second grandchild (a little girl, Elena). I ended up driving directly from the hospital to the forum.

The room was packed. There were parents, including quite a few from the city's Black community, along with a handful of teachers and two members of the school board. I thought the board members deserved credit for showing up, but both of them looked quite nervous to be there. No one from the school district administration bothered to come.

Stefanie and the NYCLU team walked people through the legal rights that systems like these violate, the ways in which the technology misidentifies people of color, and the role that student surveillance plays in what NYCLU called "the school to prison pipeline." People were attentive and asked a lot of questions. Stefanie noted afterward to the newspaper, "I'm so happy that so many community members came out. But I'm also discouraged because it's very clear the school district never answered any of these questions and didn't put out any information."

In the run-up to the meeting I was trying to figure out a simple way to explain to people how facial recognition surveillance works—how to search for specific faces it needs to scan and record all faces. One morning I looked down at the shelf where we kept our children's books and spotted the answer, *Where's Waldo?* When I pulled it out of my backpack at the forum it set off more than a few confused looks. I explained that the way you find Waldo is to study all the faces that are not Waldo and that facial recognition surveillance works the same way, in this case on our children.

Two and a half years earlier when our first granddaughter, Bella, was born I had saved a copy of the day's newspaper for her as a keepsake (the edition that ended up turning me into a local columnist). I did the same thing for little Elena as well, but hers came with something extra: a large, color frontpage photo of her Gapa holding up *Where's Waldo?*

Lawsuits, Elections, and Legislation

After the Lockport forum, Stefanie Coyle told me she had a new strategy. She wanted to have NYCLU sue the State Department of Education to force Lockport to turn the system off, and she wanted me to be the plaintiff. NYCLU felt it had a strong case against state educational officials. I liked the power of a lawsuit, but I wasn't thrilled by the idea of having my name on a legal case that my neighbors might misconstrue as me suing our local school district or trying to get money out of the deal. It did not matter that the case would be against the State Department of Education and not the Lockport School District. It did not matter that the demand of the case was getting the system turned off, not money. People who don't deal with legal actions like this one hear the word "lawsuit" and can easily misunderstand.

Nonetheless, Stefanie and NYCLU needed a genuine parent to serve as plaintiff to give the case legal standing, and I couldn't ask anyone else to do it unless I was willing to myself. This is how the case, filed in June 2020, came to be known as "Shultz et al v. New York State Department of Education." My chief co-plaintiff in the case was a powerful member of the city's Black community, Renee Cheatham.

Renee's husband, Ronald Cheatham, spent his career as a safety official at the Lockport General Motors plant. After retiring in 2012, Ron took on a different full-time job, as a peer mediator at North Park Junior High School. His role was to offer support, guidance, and conflict resolution in the complex world of preadolescents. He was charismatic and beloved by the students. Ron was also one of only a small handful of Black men employed in the entire district (none of them teachers), one with hundreds of Black students.

When Ron Cheatham turned sixty-two he went to the district administration with a request. In order to begin collecting Social Security he needed to change his job to half-time so that he wouldn't pass the federal cap on employment income. District officials turned down his request and announced that he would be leaving his post. Community reaction was swift.

In January 2020 a crowd of parents and students, many of them people of color, packed the meeting of the school board. It was an extraordinary sight in Lockport. So many people showed up to speak that the normally brief (and usually nonexistent) public comment period went on for more than forty minutes. Parents and students also presented the board with 170 letters offering similar testimonies. One of those who spoke, Cheatham's daughter Kiki, drove a straight line from that issue to another one: "It costs less than that facial recognition, I can tell you that."

From the start of the cameras controversy, Black families in Lockport were among the first to express doubts about the system. The national media was already covering three different cases of Black men falsely arrested solely on the basis of flawed facial recognition identification.[4] Many also said that they saw the facial recognition project as one more piece of a disciplinary system aimed disproportionately at their children. According to federal data, Black students in Lockport were already more than twice as likely to get suspended than white students.[5]

The school district was happy to spend $2.7 million on a system that pretended to keep children safe, but unwilling to spend $25,000 to keep a man on the job who was genuinely positioned to identify and help troubled students before any violence began. It made no sense.

I first met Renee Cheatham one evening that winter at the local Panera Bakery. She and a group of other mothers in the district were meeting to plan how to keep the pressure up on the district to keep Ron on the job. Charismatic like her husband, with a head full of long braided hair, Renee is the mother of three, deeply religious, and resolute when she sees injustice. She was also a naturally gifted organizer with a large network of friends across the city.

That following May new school board elections were coming up, and many people encouraged Renee to run. The twin controversies of the facial recognition system and the district's dismissal of a beloved peer counselor became joined together and were brewing a serious rebellion against the status quo. Renee Cheatham publicly announced that she was running and in private agreed to be a co-plaintiff in the NYCLU case over the cameras. But the formal filing of that case was still months and a school board campaign away.

Lockport's board of education election in 2020, like so many other elections in the country that year, was turned on its head by a global pandemic. The district's election in the spring turned into a preview of the complexities that would overshadow national elections that fall, enough that I wrote about it in an article for the *New York Review*: "One Small Vote for Lockport, NY, One Giant Lesson for 2020 America."

The article ran with a color photograph of students crammed into a board of education meeting to demand that Ron Cheatham be kept on the job. I wrote:

> These annual elections generally exhibit two consistent qualities: they are wickedly dull and no one shows up. In 2019, a field of four candidates running for four seats drew 856 voters from the 21,000 people registered in the school district to vote. In 2018, a hot contest with four candidates vying for three seats scored a little higher, with slightly more than 1,100 voters, a turnout just above 5 percent. Student government elections at our high school elicit more votes.

Two things changed that in 2020. One was a pandemic-driven executive order by Governor Andrew Cuomo that mandated that all the spring school elections in the state be carried out by mail only. The other was the twin controversies of the facial recognition cameras and the district's effort to get rid of Ron Cheatham. In Lockport an unprecedented field of eleven people filed as candidates for the three board seats up for election.

Renee Cheatham headed a reform slate of three candidates all of whom were Black. At the time there was not a single Black elected official anywhere in the community, despite the fact that Blacks made up nearly 10 percent of the city's population, a higher percentage than California.

In late May, just as the mail-in voting was set to begin, district residents received a small yellow postcard from the school district advising people that if they hadn't voted in any other school election in the previous four years, they were ineligible to vote in this one. It was completely untrue but with an impact that was huge. Because voter turnout in these elections never even passes the 10 percent mark, the district's bizarre voting rule would have excluded more than nine out of ten eligible voters. The postcard also came from the same school official who had led the purchase of SNTech's surveillance system, the district business manager, Deborah Coder. The result was widespread suspicion and confusion.

Fortunately, Joyce Miles, the *Union-Sun & Journal* editor, spotted the mistake and called it out on the front page. At first, district officials insisted that the requirement was real. Two days later they relented and claimed it had been a "proofreading error." The district had to spend another $8,600 to send out a correction postcard. For many, the episode had the strong smell of voter suppression in an election in which prominent Black candidates were trying to crack open an all-White board.

By election day more than fifty-three hundred people had voted, a record that outpaced the usual turnout by five-fold. So many people voted that it took school district officials three days to count all the ballots. The challengers were hopeful that the huge turnout would also mean big change. But in the end the result was much the same as always: the two incumbent board members running (status quo champions both) were returned. The exception was Renee Cheatham who came in first by a wide margin. The school board now had a genuine advocate for change in its ranks, and Lockport had its only Black elected official.

Two weeks after the votes were counted, NYCLU filed its Lockport case against the New York Department of Education, with Renee Cheatham and I as the chief plaintiffs. Our efforts to shut down Lockport's facial recognition surveillance system now turned from Lockport to Albany, both in the courts and in the State Legislature as well.

In early 2019, as national attention was beginning to focus on Lockport's high-tech school surveillance experiment, NYCLU teamed up with Democratic Assemblywoman Monica Wallace to propose legislation that would ban the use of such systems statewide in all New York schools. Wallace was from a district not far from Lockport and already familiar with the controversy. She joined forces with a Democratic state senator from New York City, Brian Kavanaugh. Their legislation made it through the State Assembly but stalled at the last minute in the Senate when time ran out on the 2019 session.

In 2020 the two state lawmakers introduced a revised bill, calling for a statewide moratorium on such systems until they could be properly studied by the State Department of Education. In the Assembly, Democratic members and Republicans alike spoke of their concerns about the potential invasions of student privacy and the predatory role of companies like SNTech that were pressing for new markets for their wares. Lockport was mentioned by one lawmaker after another. In June 2020, Wallace's bill was passed by both houses of the Legislature and signed into law by Governor Cuomo that following December.

Cuomo said in a statement, "The safety and security of our children is vital to every parent, and whether to use this technology is not a decision to be made lightly."[6] A year after the Lockport system was turned on, state law forced the district to turn it off. A New York state judge then ruled our lawsuit moot: we had already won.

The Legislature's action was a huge victory and a significant vindication of all the complaints that I and others had been making about the system for nearly three years. In the *Union-Sun & Journal*'s news report on the governor's signature I said, "The district wasted $2.7 million on a camera system that did nobody any good and was so bad that it inspired a state law."

Threatened With Arrest at a School Board Meeting

In the aftermath of the law being passed the big remaining question was whether anyone in the school district would be held accountable for such a reckless waste of $2.7 million. As far as district officials were concerned, it was all water under the bridge and something to forget. There was, however, still one more card to play.

New York state, like many states, has an obscure law that gives any citizen of the state the right to petition any agency of state government to take an action that it is authorized under state law to take. Those petitioning statutes also require those agencies to formally reply, in writing, within thirty days. By dressing up this "administrative petition" in the format of a court filing and citing that response requirement, it looks and feels like a weighty legal action, both to the agency involved and the press.

In February 2021 I filed a formal petition with the office of New York State Comptroller Thomas DiNapoli, requesting that the state audit the Lockport district's purchase of its facial recognition system, citing a list of apparent irregularities. To my surprise, a month later, the comptroller announced that he was initiating that audit. The announcement made the front page of the *Buffalo News*.[7]

Lockport district officials insisted publicly that the comptroller's announcement was pure coincidence, and Superintendent Bradley doubled down on a lie that would come back to haunt her badly: "Despite repeated incorrect claims to the contrary, the fact is that the Aegis System was purchased through a competitive bidding process."

A year later, in April 2022, the comptroller's office completed its hard look into the district's actions. The report was twenty-three pages long and deeply detailed. Its conclusions were devastating for the school district and Superintendent Bradley. The comptroller's office wrote: "The District sought no competition prior to awarding the facial recognition software license agreement but, nonetheless expressly suggested that a competitive process was issued by the District for the facial recognition software. It is our view [this] misled the public to believe the District sought competition for the facial recognition software license agreement, when in fact, no such competition had been sought."

The audit was a genuine smoking gun of deliberate fiscal mismanagement. My column in the *Union-Sun & Journal* the next week was titled, "Financial Malpractice in Lockport Schools": "Superintendent Michelle Bradley, district business manager Deborah Coder, and district technology director Rob LiPuma—the team that brought the facial recognition project to the district—are three of the highest paid public servants in Western New York. Did they really not understand that you don't spend that kind of money on anything without comparing offers from different companies first?"

I went the next week once more to the meeting of the Lockport Board of Education and used the public comment period to go through the audit in detail and confront school officials with what the comptroller had found. I asked the board, "What are you going to do about the fact that we have a superintendent who lies to the public about a $2.7 million project?"

It was an intense moment, and when I hit my three-minute time limit the new board president, Karen Young, told me to end my comments. I refused, telling board members that you could not summarize a twenty-three-page, year-long audit in 180 seconds and I kept talking. That is when all hell broke loose.

Young gaveled the session over. She directed all of the members to join her in a retreat to a back room for an executive session. She directed the operators of the community access channel to turn off their cameras. A few minutes later a school security officer came out and told me that if I did not back away from the microphone immediately he was going to call the Lockport Police Department and have me arrested for trespassing.

All of this commotion happened right in front of the new reporter for the *Union-Sun & Journal* (Connor Hoffman had left Lockport to attend law school) who was there to cover the meeting for the paper. The next day the story was splashed across the front page of the paper, with a photo of me speaking to the board and the headline, "Lockport School Board Walks Out on Speaker":

> A longtime critic of facial recognition technology and its procurement by the Lockport City School District from SN Technologies, as well as a grandparent of a child in the school district, Jim Shultz, stood in front of the Board of Education Wednesday night with a laundry list of complaints. Chief among them was the district's spending of $2.7 million on a technology which a state law ultimately banned the use of.
>
> While Shultz continued to speak at Wednesday's meeting, the board walked out of the room because Shultz went over his 3-minute time limit to speak despite numerous calls to stop by board President Karen Young. Dennis Sobieraski, a security guard, then appeared and told Shultz that unless he stopped talking, he'd be forced to call the police and pursue charges of trespass.
>
> Jill Caruso, a mother of a student in the district who had offered to give her time to speak to Shultz but was denied that option by Young. 'What I just witnessed is amazing to me,' she said. 'You should've sat here. You should've listened. Caruso went on to say that not listening to Shultz was an act of 'cowardice."

I had no plan to instigate such drama, but it taught me one more lesson about the small town I lived in: actions definitely speak louder than words and almost getting arrested at a school board meeting got everyone's attention. More than 150 people weighed in on the story on the Lockportians Facebook page, and they all had a similar tenor:

"If they get away with it once they'll do it again, it needs to be addressed."

"The Superintendent gets paid and paid well. She would be fired working in private sector. What was done (misleading us taxpayers) is fraud and criminal."

"In my opinion, if anyone is to be censured, it is whoever was responsible for accepting a bid without it being put out for bid to other companies."

"My daughter's teachers at middle school want my 13 year old to be accountable for not turning in assignments, so why isn't the Superintendent and the Board accountable for this action. It's criminal."

Offline, reaction was just as intense. For days, everywhere I went people I didn't know stopped me and wanted to talk about what happened and offer their support. More than once while I was riding my bike, a perfect stranger in a car would slow down beside me, roll down the window, and offer their appreciation. My neighbor called me over to the fence one afternoon to express his disgust at how I was treated. An elderly couple in line with me at a local ice cream parlor told me they had watched the video recording of the meetings four times. A grandmother at the playground where I was pushing my youngest granddaughter on the swings came up to me and asked with a grin, "So, did they let you out on bail?"

At the next public board meeting I went back and directly called on Superintendent Bradley to resign or be fired. A month later, Bradley announced suddenly that she was leaving her post, well before the end of her $200,000 per year contract. She said that she was leaving to take a position that she had been offered somewhere else but declined to say what it was. No one was really fooled.

Two Steps Forward and One Step Back

Under significant public scrutiny at this point, the Lockport Board of Education surveyed the community about what it wanted in a new school district superintendent and carried out a national search. In January 2023 it announced its selection, Dr. Mathis Calvin III. Calvin was the popular superintendent of a smaller district in a different part of Western New York. Calvin is also Black, which was an extraordinary leap forward for a school district that didn't even have a single Black male teacher in any school.

At a community event to introduce him, Dr. Calvin spoke of his desire for an open and transparent administration of Lockport's schools. He said that his door was open to anyone in the community who wanted to talk, and he meant it. We spent an hour together soon after he took over, and he asked the kind of questions about the district that up to then had been nearly ignored. The difference in style with his predecessor could not have been starker.

A few months later, in May 2023, the school district once again faced a significantly contested election for Board of Education. Seven candidates were running for three seats. This included Renee Cheatham running for a second term. It seemed like the momentum for change in the district was moving forward after years of being stuck under the thumb of an old guard. But the old guard had other plans.

The Lockport Educators' Association, the teachers' union, still essentially called the shots in board elections. When only about one in ten voters bother to show up, having a big block of teachers and their families loyally voting for whomever the LEA endorsed made all the difference, and the union's apparent mantra was never rock the boat. The LEA endorsed three candidates, all white men. It didn't even offer to interview any of the women running or the people of color, including Renee.

Backed by union phone banks and mailers, the three men endorsed by the LEA won. Renee came in fourth. I could hear the deep disappointment in her voice when we spoke afterward. She had worked hard and had been brave and the old guard of the district was eager to see her go.

At the state level, meanwhile, in August 2023, the New York Office of Information Technology Assessment finally released its long-awaited study mandated by the Lockport-inspired state law freezing the use of systems like these statewide. The report concluded that, despite all the boasts made by the companies about how facial recognition systems could make schools safer, there was no actual evidence to support the claim and plenty to demonstrate its potential risks.

A month later New York's state commissioner of education issued an executive order banning the use of the technology in all of the state's public and private schools, more than six thousand of them. The system launched in a tiny corner of Western New York six years earlier had sparked a national movement and now a full ban across the fourth largest state in the country. The headline in the *Buffalo News* used a quote I had given the reporter, Stupid from the Beginning.

In the end, that was the thing that really stopped the deployment of facial recognition in schools. What won the day, in Lockport and beyond, was not an argument from either the left or the right. It was an argument about common sense. The people I had come to know in Lockport, of whatever political stripe, prided themselves on being practical and good at spotting foolishness. Lockport's infamous spy cameras had become such a huge issue because the whole project just seemed genuinely stupid. School officials didn't do their homework and then lied about it when they got caught.

It made me understand that common sense might actually be an ideology that could bring otherwise divided people together.

Chapter Three

Black in Lockport

A few weeks after our arrival in Lockport, I was riding my bicycle down South Street just behind the old Harrison Radiator factory. The building is almost a full block long, constructed of century-old brick and aging glass windows. It had once been the center of Lockport's economic life, but that summer it stood mostly empty, except for a small group of organizations and businesses that have set up shop on its second floor. Across the street sits a row of small homes built in the early 1900s, many in various states of disrepair. A significant portion of Lockport's Black community lives in this neighborhood.

The little boy who yelled out to me was probably seven years old and Black. "Look out, there is a car behind you," he shouted. I thanked him and pedaled onward. It took me about three seconds to realize that I had misheard him. He had not yelled out, "Look out, there is *a car* behind you." He had warned me, "Look out, there is *a cop* behind you." Sure enough as I turned around I saw a Lockport Police Department cruiser right behind me.

What was it, I wondered, that made such a young child so afraid of the police? Was it an actual experience of his own? Was it from what he overheard in the conversations of adults? I felt certain that a White child that age in Lockport would not have yelled out such a warning as I rode by.

Lockport's population is mostly White, about 80 percent of its residents according to the most recent census. The city, however, is also home to a sizeable Black community, one with a long and deep history here. In 2020 Blacks accounted for just over 10 percent of the city's population, a portion nearly double that of California.

When the history is told about the construction of the Erie Canal in the 1820s, the characters at the center are usually immigrant men from Ireland who came to build an epic waterway and then stayed to build a thriving town. The other, less talked about labor force that built that canal in the middle of nowhere comprised Black men who traveled here from places like New York City. Those builders of history also included runaway slaves. In fact, the canal itself became a part of the underground railroad that helped many of those slaves escape to freedom.[1]

In the decades that followed, Lockport's Black community continued as a powerful force, helping shape the city that it is today. A Black brickmaker would lead a winning campaign to integrate the city's schools nearly a century before the nation did. Black workers would help build Harrison Radiator into an industrial force. A thriving neighborhood where Black families and Italian families intermingled would spread out across lower town below the canal, a place complete with its own stores, schools, and barber shops.

By 2017 that neighborhood had been destroyed by Urban Renewal, and those families were scattered to the winds. Harrison Radiator was gone, and the GM plant that replaced it employed only a small fraction as many workers. The history-making achievements in education were replaced by a school district with not a single Black male teacher. Then, in 2019, Lockport would also become yet one more city where a Black man was killed by White police officers.

The Death of Troy Hodge

Lockport's relationship with its Black community changed in a tragic instant on June 16, 2019. That was the night that Troy Hodge, a thirty-nine-year-old Black man who had lived in Lockport his whole life, died in the hands of four White officers with the Lockport Police Department and Niagara County Sheriff. The precise events of that night were pieced together only slowly, through the investigative efforts of journalists and of the New York State Attorney General.[2]

Shortly before midnight, Hodge's mother, Fatima Hodge, made a series of calls to 911 asking for help. Her son, she said, was not himself. As the result of a previous automobile accident, Hodge had been prescribed opioids and battled with addiction issues for years afterward. The same pain management specialist who gave Hodge his medications was later prosecuted by state officials for over-prescription. His mother said his medications were making him act strangely.

When Lockport officers arrived they found both mother and son to be "visibly upset." Hodge reportedly said he was going into his house to get a shotgun. The officers stopped him by pulling him from the back of his sweatshirt. This turned into a physical struggle between Hodge and two police officers. According to the attorney general's report, Hodge had some kind of knife in one of his hands. Whether it was anything more than an unopened pocketknife remains unclear. One of the officers used her taser gun on Hodge. In response Hodge reportedly tried to bite another officer. The struggle between Hodge and what became four police officers lasted for nearly ten minutes until officers subdued him to the ground.

In a video taken by a bystander across the street with a mobile phone, Hodge can be heard yelling out repeatedly, "Mom, don't let them kill me. Don't let them kill me." Minutes later Hodge stopped moving entirely. His mother frantically asked officers if her son was dead. "No. He's not dead. He's fine," one officer told her.

According to state records, it was just after that when Hodge's breathing stopped and police could not find a pulse. An ambulance finally arrived on the scene to take Hodge to the emergency room at the Lockport Hospital. At 12:40 a.m., an hour after Hodge's mother had first called 911 for help, her son was pronounced dead.

Lockport's Black community is close knit, and the Hodge family is well-known here. They have lived in their small house on Park Avenue for more than forty years. Fatima Hodge, a deeply religious woman, is an active member of her church, Latter Rain Cathedral. In the community she is known simply as "Mother Hodge." Her son Troy was a graduate of Lockport High School. Afterward he worked in construction. Many local friends were quick to remember him as polite and caring. His extended family of aunts, uncles, and cousins ran through the city. Hodge and his longtime girlfriend, Nicole Calamita, had a fourteen-year-old daughter, Tamara. She was a grade behind our daughter Mariana at Lockport High.

Reaction to Hodge's death was swift and vehement, but it was peaceful. People wanted answers. Why did a mother's plea for help turn into her son's death? What had the police done to provoke a tragedy that seemed so needless, for his family and for the whole community?

Hodge's death took place in the early hours of Monday morning. On the Wednesday afternoon afterward the Lockport Common Council called its regularly scheduled meeting to order at City Hall, just five blocks from where Hodge had died in police hands.

Dozens of city residents, mostly Black, joined in a rally just outside.[3] They carried signs and wore newly made shirts that read JUSTICE FOR TROY.

Afterward the protesters crowded into the council chambers where members were listening to a bureaucratic presentation about property tax exemptions.

Mayor Michelle Roman saw the moment for what it was and understood that Hodge's death and the community's demand for answers took priority. The Council's meeting was converted into a two-hour forum on the behavior of the Lockport police and what had happened just two days before. Chief of Police Steven Preisch and County District Attorney Caroline Wojtaszek were summoned from their nearby offices to answer questions.

"A mother called for help with her son and he was killed," said one family friend, Kimberly Jenkins, who had helped organize the rally. "Things like that shouldn't happen. People in the community want answers." One Black resident after another spoke of their own abusive experiences with the Lockport Police Department. Several also reminded city leaders that the department had not a single Black officer in its ranks of more than forty.

"Protocol needs to be changed regarding people with mental health issues," Jenkins told the officials.

In the days after Hodge's death, the community rallied around his family and held a fundraiser to help with the costs of his burial. I rode my bike over to the large gathering at a park alongside the Erie Canal. Close to a hundred people came together for an afternoon of homemade food sold to benefit the Hodges. I was struck though by how little support seemed to be coming from beyond the Black community. Was this one more sign of Lockport's lines of segregation?

Walking through the crowd without fanfare was Mayor Roman. One of the few Democrats in local office at the time, Roman is a middle school teacher. Her opponent had said during the campaign that she was too much a political amateur to lead the city. Her handling of the Hodge case, however, showed what a natural and competent leader she was. I asked her once in an interview how teaching middle schoolers prepared someone to be mayor. She told me that in one way it is the same. "You walk in the door every morning and you never know what surprises are going to come." I don't think she ever imagined she would be leading the city through a crisis like Troy Hodge's death.

The answers that the community wanted about Hodge's death would end up being more than two years away. Under New York state law, the investigation of any death involving the police is automatically moved into the hands of the state attorney general, and the attorney general's office moved slowly.

In the meantime, however, it was clear that something deeper had changed in the city as a whole. The issue of police abuse was now a public conversation. The Black community in Lockport was speaking out in a way that felt more determined and resolute. The Lockportians Facebook group, usually filled with posts about lost cats and potholes, became filled with something else as well—expressions of pain and anger from the city's Black residents. The question was whether the White community in Lockport was actually listening.

"Black in Lockport"

A few weeks after Hodge's death I went to Joyce Miles, the newspaper's editor, with an idea. I wanted to do a handful of in-depth interviews with Black residents of the city about their experiences living in Lockport, and I wanted to turn it into a series of columns. I asked her what she thought. Joyce was supportive from the start, and she suggested an alternative, a series of articles not on the opinion page but on the newspaper's front page.

I knew going into it what a presumptive project it was. I was White, I was new to the community, and my connections with Blacks in Lockport were as thin as you could get. Who was I to pick who would speak for that community? Who was I to decide what part of what people said would go into the paper and what part would be left unpublished? But I felt that there was an opening that was important to take.

I reached out with an appeal to the Lockportians group on Facebook. I explained my intention for the series and asked if there were members of the city's Black community willing to speak with me. Four powerful people, of different ages and different backgrounds, reached back out to me eager to talk. I set times with each of them to meet over a coffee and also arranged for the newspaper photographer to meet them for a photo.

The series ran three days in a row the first week of September under the title "Black in Lockport." In the first article I shared my story of the little boy who had warned me about a police cruiser driving behind me, and I explained that the motivation behind the series came from the aftermath of Troy Hodge's killing. Then I introduced the four people who had agreed to speak for the series and a brief preview of what each had to say:

> Jayde McDonald is 22, a lifelong Lockportian, a 2015 graduate of Lockport High School, and currently an honors student in political science at Buffalo State:
> "My brother had a White friend and she would always call the house and they would talk and hang out and the mother

found out that my brother was Black and called the house and spoke to my mom and said, 'I don't want my daughter associating with you people,' and hung up. My brother was in the seventh or eighth grade."

Kandyce Cauley is 27, also a Lockport native and a graduate of LHS. She works as a team leader at General Motors:

"I think [a White person] doesn't know how uncomfortable it is. When a White person walks into an all-Black function or restaurant they feel that right away. But they don't have to walk into an all-Black restaurant. They don't have to walk into a restaurant owned by Black people. They don't have to do that. I have to walk into an all-White restaurant because that's where I live. Those are my only options."

Will King is 38 and a personal fitness trainer. He was raised in Lockport, moved away for a time to Medina, and then returned with his family to make the city his home once more:

"On Continental Drive [a White neighborhood] a cop will pull over to the side and say, 'Hey I see you got a new truck. How much did that set you back?' It's a conversation. That same cop comes down to Washburn [a Black neighborhood] and if he pulls you over he's asking you for your license and registration and he's asking you 'How did you get that truck?'"

Mark Sanders is 49 and has been the pastor at Refuge Temple of Christ church for 21 years. He also serves as the community policing liaison with Lockport Police Department.

"An African American child in Lockport sees nothing of success in themselves, whether it be a fireman, a police officer, a public official, a principal, they see nothing. What does that psychologically do to a child when the only thing you see in the paper is who got arrested? It's great when you are a White child and everywhere you go you see what you can be, doctors, dentists, lawyers, judges."

In the installments that followed, the four of them shared painful stories of what it was like to grow up and live in a community where they were always in the minority and always looked at differently.

Will King: "There is always that color when it comes to Black folks. But when they describe somebody of White descent they never say White."

JAYDE MCDONALD: "I grew up until maybe sophomore year in high school hating my skin color because my peers' parents were never OK with me going into their home because they feared I might steal something or disrespect their house. If we are in a store we get followed. Especially because my mom is White and she's short whenever we walk into a situation everyone stops their conversation and stares. Even if I hung out with a White girl for the first time I would always ask, 'Are your parents OK with Black people? Like have you ever had a Black person in your house?' It's so heavy because what if they see me and they say, you can't come in."

KANDYCE CAULEY: "We definitely had a super sense of separation, maybe even a feeling of inferiority. The eyes weren't on you for good things but they were on you for negative things. People not expecting you to be as good as your peers. People expecting negative things from you. Black people have to be better to prove themselves and White people don't really have to prove themselves. They just are better because of what they look like."

MARK SANDERS: "Your color is something you can't hide and this is a predominantly White city. People are still driven by stereotypes. There is still a fear factor. I think there are still people who fear African Americans."

They talked about the feeling of always being the outsider:

KANDYCE: "It's a feeling that I have to prove myself whenever I am around people who don't look like me, which is exhausting. I always have a feeling of being uncomfortable when I go out in public. There is always less of me than there are of other people. I have never been anywhere in this city to eat or any bar in this city to have a drink anywhere where I feel like there are as many people who look like me as look like the White community. Never, it's never happened. I've lived in this city for 27 years and I still walk in places and feel like people are looking at me like, 'Well, what are you doing here?'"

MARK: "There aren't a lot of places outside the school system where we mix. There are some businesses here that I've never seen an African American working in, even low-level jobs like for teenagers. Pizza parlors and things like that. You have a school system where there is very nil representation of African Americans. You have a government that has zero representation. Compound all of that together and it's the feeling of being disenfranchised."

In the final article in the series, I asked the four about their experiences with the public schools and with the Lockport police.

"I was friends with a lot of the rich White people but we never hung out outside of school," explained Jayde. "It was only like in-school friendships. And the people I met with outside the school were my Black best friends. I had one White best friend but he was gay and he knew what it was like. That's the only place we talked, hung out, in the high school. I don't know if it has to do with money or with color."

"I was a student athlete," remembered Kandyce. "I was like a chameleon, you know, jumping into the skin that you need to when you are around certain people. It was still exhausting for me. It's the feeling of not being 100% you 98% of the time. I may have been the only Black girl on my basketball team most of the time but I wouldn't hang out with any of those girls if I wasn't on the team with them."

Will told me, "You have teachers who automatically assume. Let's say Jamal acts up in school and no one asks why Jamal is acting up in school, he just gets suspended. But if John acts up the same way we're going to have a teachers' meeting and get to the bottom of it. There are two different avenues always."

Mark Sanders, who does workshops with students at the high school, told me, "You have kids who have yachts and you have kids that have never seen the water. You have poor kids who can't relate to, 'We're going to Disney World for vacation.' You also have kids who can't relate to, 'My mother was locked up and we were here for five days by ourselves.' The administration and teachers sometimes can't relate to these kids."

My interviews came at a time when the issue of police violence aimed at Black people was exploding around the country, and just months after Hodge's killing in Lockport.

Jayde told me, "The first time I was pulled over I started crying because I did not know what to do. I don't want them to hurt me. I don't want anything bad to happen. I remember being terrified and that is always on my mind." She called the death of Troy Hodge heartbreaking. "Imagine you being a mother, calling the police to help your son and he dies in front of you. It makes me scared for my family, my brother especially who is my best friend."

"I knew Troy personally," Kandyce told me. "I'm surprised that it was him but I'm not surprised that happened. His mother is a staple in this community and the church community. I think if those officers knew them personally they would have handled it differently. But they don't take the time as a police department to know the people that they're working with."

Mark, who works as the community liaison to Lockport Police Department, told me about what he called the ritual of degradation, "One of the things that a lot of police officers don't understand is the fear factor. When you get cuffed and those lights come on, those things you have to do, get down on the ground. I don't care who you are. If I see lights behind me, I panic." He also added, "I also want people also to see the human side of them [Lockport police]. They are not every YouTube video you've watched. Just like as an African American I don't want to be stereotyped, let's give them the same regard, to know them as individuals."

Reaction to the series came in many ways. As I traveled around town in the days afterward, several people stopped to thank me for writing it and said that it had opened their eyes. A local surgeon in town, who along with his wife was a staple of the city's establishment, approached me and asked what they could do to help stimulate more conversations across Lockport's racial divide.

Others were not so pleased. An angry reader of the paper emailed the editor, "As a believer of freedom of speech, this Black article isn't freedom of speech. It's hate speech and discrimination now on Lockport's homepage."

But it was in the Lockportians Facebook group where the reaction was most intense after I posted the series there. There were nearly two hundred comments. Some readers, all of them White, attacked me for writing it and the paper for publishing it:

"I believe articles of this kind only further the racial divide."

"Creating division much these days Jim ???"

"Yes, it helped fill some pages on that rag . . . they are going to lose a lot of the few subscribers they have."

One reader said that I needed to do a series about the experience of being White in Lockport, "Why just Blacks?"

There were also comments from people in the Black community who wanted to make it quite clear that racism in Lockport was real and to recount some of their own hard experiences:

> "It is sad sitting here and seeing how everyone is saying there ain't a problem. Well let me tell you what happened to me and my sister and our kids the one day we went to Denny's. We are standing there waiting to be seated. Now us just standing there doing nothing wrong mind you . . . this old man walks by and says move your n***** kids. I was so heartbroken sad and mad all at the same time like what did my kids do so wrong to be called names like that."

There were quite a few readers, both White and Black, who saw the series as an important expression of the city's racial realities.

> "I am really absolutely disgusted with all of you pretending that racist bullshit doesn't happen here in Lockport. If you honestly believe this then you need to look at yourself and how you're contributing to it."

> "There's a quiet majority who will never comment on social media who are very glad that this three part series was written. If it sparks even a handful of people to reflect inwardly then I would think that is a measure of success."

> "I have lived here all my life and have never heard this perspective before."

In the aftermath of Troy Hodge's killing race was starting to become an issue talked about much more openly in Lockport, especially as specific issues that touched on race continued to surface over and over. The next place that happened was a familiar one, the bungled affairs of the Lockport School District.

My Brother's Keeper

In February 2012, Trayvon Martin, a seventeen-year-old unarmed high school student, was shot and killed in Florida by a Neighborhood Watch volunteer. He was killed because he was young and Black and wearing a hoodie as he walked to a local convenience store. That was enough to trigger another man's prejudice and fear to carry out murder. It was a death that resonated deeply in the Black community, from family tables to the White House.

"When I think about this boy," said President Barack Obama, "I think about my own kids and I think every parent in America should be able to understand why it is absolutely imperative that we investigate every aspect of this. If I had a son he would look like Trayvon."

Two years later the president launched an initiative from the White House called My Brother's Keeper. He called it, "an all-hands-on-deck, comprehensive approach to breaking down some of the barriers and stereotypes and racist presumptions that so often put Black boys and boys of color in vulnerable positions." After leaving office he continued the program through the Obama Foundation. This included a whole set of mentoring programs and other projects to lift up the lives of boys and young men of color.

In 2016, the State of New York decided to initiate its own My Brother's Keeper program. State lawmakers created a $20 million budget to support projects statewide, aimed to support boys and young men of color. A large portion of those funds were distributed to school districts with significant populations of students of color, districts like Lockport (where students of color are nearly one out of five).[4]

And just as with the facial recognition cameras before, the leadership of the Lockport School District went after a giant state grant with big implications for the district's students and never bothered to consult with anyone in the community about it beforehand. In fact, they kept it a closely guarded secret.

In the spring of 2021 I got a phone call from Renee Cheatham, who had now served almost a full year on the Lockport Board of Education. She invited me to a meeting of people from the Black community to talk about the district's My Brother's Keeper plans. Even though she was a member of the Board of Education she hadn't heard about the project until after the district superintendent, Michelle Bradley, had written and submitted a $500,000 plan to the state for funding. The group that met that afternoon in a local park had no illusions. They knew that the school district had left them out of the planning on purpose. The reasons why were clear from how the project was designed.

The My Brother's Keeper program is supposed to target support to boys and young men of color because they are such an at-risk group. The district's proposal made no mention of such targeting. The project was

Black in Lockport | 61

supposed to assemble a coalition of community partners to help shape it. The district had done nothing of the sort. In fact, it never even bothered to reach out to organizations in the community already doing exactly this kind of mentoring work with young people of color.

The ad hoc group that met in the park that afternoon decided to call a community meeting and ask the superintendent and other school officials to attend. On a Monday evening in mid-June, two dozen people gathered in the pews of the Latter Rain Cathedral, the predominantly Black church on the city's west side. The only school official present was Renee Cheatham. But a reporter for the *Union-Sun & Journal* was there and reported the story on the front page the next day.

Teria Young, a mother who had also previously served as vice-president of the Lockport High School PTA, said, "They got the grant and they want to tell us what needs to be done in our community."

Another mother, Paula Travis, warned about the district's plan to put armed security guards in school buildings. "These men they are talking about are not actually current police officers, these are retired, suspended, fired. They are security guards, that's it. For them to walk around carrying a gun?"

Later that week I published a column titled, "The Lockport School District Must Listen to Black Families." I wrote: "The Lockport district applied for and won a $500,000 grant from the New York State Education Department to start a My Brother's Keeper program in our schools. That's fine, but the district never bothered to consult with any Black parents or students about what kind of program we should have. In fact, it seems like the district tried to keep the whole thing a secret."

On the same day that my column appeared in the newspaper I received an email from Dr. Anael Alston, the New York Department of Education's Assistant Commissioner for Access, Equity, and Community Engagement Services. New York's My Brother's Keeper program was under his jurisdiction. Dr. Alston wrote that he had read my column and asked if we could set up a time to talk by phone. When we spoke the following week, he listened to the story about how the school district had failed to consult with anyone in the community. At one point he interrupted and asked, "Wait a minute, back-up. Are you telling me that the school district didn't even bother to consult beforehand with the only person of color on the board of education [Renee Cheatham]?" I told him that was exactly what had happened. He replied, "Ok, I think I need to pay a visit to Lockport."

Dr. Alston's visit was scheduled for August and as soon as word got out the Lockport District decided to try to get ahead of things. District officials announced a plan to have a special community forum on the My Brother's Keep Project as part of their July school board meeting and hold that forum in the large Lockport High auditorium rather than the small district board room with few seats.

This was a highly unusual step for the school board to take and it would have been difficult for district officials to screw it up worse.

The district published a sharp start time for the forum at 6 p.m. and that was when about two dozen people, most of them Black parents and grandparents, promptly arrived and took their seats. People told me that they had arranged for special babysitters or skipped out on making their family's dinner in order to be there. At almost 7 p.m. we were all still waiting for the school board members and administrators to emerge from a closed-door executive session in some unidentified room in another part of the building.

As people voiced their frustration, several decided that it was time to go find the board and tell them it was time to start. No one in the auditorium looked more bored waiting for the forum to begin than James Neiss, the veteran photographer for the newspaper. He seemed to be using the extra time in his seat for a short nap. I told him, "Hey Jim, you might want to follow those people. I think you will have your front page photo for tomorrow." A group of about half a dozen parents roamed around the halls until they found the classroom with a windowless door and voices coming from inside.

A father in a t-shirt that said FIGHT RACISM politely knocked on the door until a very surprised Board of Education president, Karen Young, finally opened it. The front page photo in the next day's paper showed her with that same surprised face and the backs of Black parents who stood facing her. The newspaper's article, by reporter Benjamin Joe, was titled, "Frustrated Parents Confront Lockport School Board on My Brother's Keeper Grant."

> A small crowd, who'd been kept waiting for more than an hour, finally knocked on the door where the school board members were deliberating in executive session and demanded they come back to the auditorium and continue the meeting.
>
> "You got to do executive session later," Teria Young, a Black mother with children in the school district said. "You've got people waiting here, and this is ridiculous."

The board quickly moved to the auditorium and began the forum, starting with a presentation by the district's grant writer, Holly Dickerson. When asked why she hadn't bothered to consult with anyone in the community who actually worked with children and young people of color, she explained, "They just aren't in my professional network." It was a beautifully clean example of how racism gets built into a public institution. A project for Black families was designed without Black families because the White professional designing the project said she didn't know any.

Then the board heard from one parent after another. The newspaper quoted several:

> "How many times in the past have you people lied to get money by saying you want to help us?" Steve Huston asked. "Somebody should be prosecuted; somebody should go to jail. That whole thing with the My Brother's Keeper grant. You people had no intention of communicating with the Black community. You did what you wanted to do."
>
> Tara Clayton, another Black mother, also spoke. "I, too, am a mother of three Black sons, two have graduated from Lockport School District, one who will be a senior in September and I have Black grandchildren who will be attending this district. The only representation I see for my grandchildren is Mrs. Cheatham. I don't understand how any of you can sit there, in good conscious, and try to present this grant knowing you did not follow any of these guidelines."

Under heavy pressure for her second mishandling of a major state grant, Superintendent Bradley announced that the plan submitted to the state probably needed to be scrapped and "started over from scratch." People in the auditorium applauded.

Dr. Alston arrived in Lockport a few weeks later. Having an assistant state commissioner of education come to town was a big event for a small city. He met with the top district administrators, held a special session with the board of education, and then an open forum for the community in the same church where people had gathered two months earlier. This time the pews were packed.

Dr. Alston's chastisement of the school board was diplomatic but clear. "Our assessment was that the community engagement part, before they sent it in, could've been better. I think everyone knows that. Otherwise, I wouldn't be here."[5]

Over the course of the next few months, and under the watchful eye of the State Department of Education, the district assembled a community advisory committee to oversee the project. It included a majority of Black members including several people who had been the project's vocal critics. The project also eventually initiated a youth mentoring program led by a pair of African American men with deep local roots, as well as a Nurturing Fathers program for young dads.

The process was not without bumps, but the voices of those on the committee had weight now. The city's African American community was finding a more public voice and Lockport's attention to matters of race was changing, but slowly.

The Powerful Lockport Legacy of Aaron Mossell

Among the nation's current social divisions, one that has sparked some of the most heated and emotional debate is the question of how we should remember our country's history. This includes, especially, how we talk about race and the layers of deep injustice that have defined our history and still shape the nation's reality today. Here again, Lockport has a story to tell that is as big as the country but as local as one middle school—a decades-long effort to honor the legacy of a home-grown Black education pioneer.

Aaron Mossell was born in Baltimore in 1824. As a young married man with children in the 1850s, he and his family lived under the constant fear of being mistaken for and captured as runaway slaves under the Fugitive Slave Act passed by Congress. In 1856 the Mossel family finally fled to Canada where they could live away from such fears and remained there until the end of the US Civil War a decade later. That is when the Mossells returned to the US and settled themselves in the small, bustling town beside the Erie Canal, named for the locks that raised and lowered the barges passing through it.

As his great-granddaughter, Dr. Rae Alexander-Minter, recounts the history, Mossell set up a new brickmaking business near the center of the city and did very well. But she says that always, his true passion was education. As another of his descendants, Dr. Forrester Lee, told me, "For those who struggled in life, and particularly those who were enslaved, education was the way to a better life."

One of Mossell's sons, Charles, became a well-known local pastor at Lockport's First African Methodist Episcopal Church. "But like his father, he was deeply troubled by the inequities of a socio-economic and political system that denied equal access and opportunity for African Americans," said Alexander-Minter.

Lockport's city schools, like most in America after the Civil War, were segregated by race, with Black children receiving a far inferior quality of education. The Reverend Mossell went to the Lockport Board of Education with a demand that the city's schools be integrated. The board hemmed and hawed and stalled, but it did not budge.

In response, in January 1873, his father the brickmaker called together a meeting of the city's Black families. Hundreds turned out at and took a decision together to boycott and sit-in at the Black schools. According to his great-granddaughter's telling of the story, Mossell and the Black community's fight for integrated schools took three years before it was won. A turning point was when Mossell offered school officials bricks for construction of a new school, but only if the district was integrated.

White school officials finally relented and in 1876 the Lockport schools became officially integrated nearly eighty years before that would be achieved nationwide with the US Supreme Court's history-making 1954 ruling in *Brown vs. the Board of Topeka*.

The story of Aaron Mossell and the battle to integrate the city's schools was known in Lockport but not widely. A small, nondescript metal plaque was erected in his honor in a lost corner of a city park, but that was about it. A group of local residents, Black and White both, along with a few of Mossell's descendants, set their sights on a different and more visible honor, one that would make his legacy known to each new generation.

For the Mossell family, no aspect of his legacy was more profound than the brickmaker's deep commitment to education. This was reflected not just in his historic efforts at desegregation but in the long legacy of the Mossell family and one ground-breaking Ivy League education after another. Dr. Alexander-Minter, his great-granddaughter, is a nationally renowned anthropologist at Columbia University. Her father was one of the first Black graduates of Harvard Law School. Her mother was the first Black woman lawyer in Pennsylvania. Dr. Lee, his great-grandson, is a retired professor from the Yale University School of Medicine.

By elegant coincidence, Lockport's North Park Junior High sat on the exact same parcel of land that was once home to Aaron Mossell's brickmaking business. For those looking to recognize his legacy in a lasting way, renaming the school in his honor was a perfect fit, both in meaning and location. But getting the modern-day Lockport Board of Education to see it that way proved to be an even longer struggle than Mossell's to win integration from the 1870s Board of Education a century and a half before.

The proposal to rename the school after Mossell was first made in 2006 and gained no traction with the city's school board. It was reproposed over and over, each time without success. As late as 2014 the Lockport Board of Education continued to reject it. Board members claimed that the community was just too deeply attached to the name North Park to part with it (even though the school was named after a park that did not actually exist). Dr. Lee offered me a different explanation, "The reason it was turned down is because the city didn't think it had a racial problem in the past."

Nonetheless, in an echo of Mossell's previous efforts, the citizens and family members behind the name change were persistent, and in 2021 that renaming was finally approved. It was propelled in part by the increasing attention on racial injustice around the nation in the aftermath of the 2020 police killing of George Floyd and new attention locally in the aftermath of Troy Hodge's killing by police in Lockport. The district's own series of missteps on issues related to race likely had an impact as well. The arc of history finally bent to honor Lockport's own hero for racial justice.

In September 2021 as the new school year was set to begin, a gathering of all colors came together on a sunny afternoon to witness the formal renaming of the school in Mossell's honor. A giant construction crane was used to hoist and mount his name in huge white letters to the school's tall red brick front. The ceremony featured Boy Scouts and the school band and all the good trappings of a small-town event.

Mayor Roman told those gathered, "His name will now be known and what he did for the community will now be known." School board member Renee Cheatham said joyously, "My heart is just full, this is something that should've happened a long time ago." Dr. Alexander-Minter, who traveled from New York City to speak at the ceremony, told me afterward, "Young people, White, Black, Brown and Asian, need to know this story. It takes a long time to make change. We know that."

In the week before the renaming I wrote my own column about the event and its meaning: "Mossell's great grandson told me that the renaming is actually less about his family than it is about Lockport coming to terms with its own history. 'I think history helps form the present and propels the future,' he said. The renaming ceremony this week is about a man and a community's struggle for civil rights a century and a half ago. But that history does directly speak to the present." To be clear, not everyone in Lockport was happy with the school's name change. A local man named Garth Wilson sent a letter to the newspaper expressing a view I heard more than once. "The Lockport school board had no reason to rename North Park to Aaron Mossell Junior High School. For decades, North End families sent their kids to North Park. My kids and neighbors' kids went there. Now, pressured by a few, they thought that the school should be awarded a Black person's name."

There it was in microcosm, the national debate about remembering history for what it was and also the resentment from those who don't like the changes that come with it.

A Racist Massacre Hits Home

Tops Market is a modest-sized regional chain of grocery stores in and around Buffalo, New York. Lockport has two of them. The Tops store on Jefferson Avenue in Buffalo is a thirty-minute drive away in the heart of the city's Black neighborhood. One of its security guards was fifty-five-year-old Aaron Salter Jr., a former Buffalo Police lieutenant and a resident of Lockport. Salter was a well-known and well-liked figure in Lockport, the father of three children who enjoyed working on motorcycle engines as a hobby.

Salter was the guard on duty on the afternoon of Saturday, May 14, 2022. That was the day an eighteen-year-old who had just finished writing a 180-page racist manifesto drove halfway across the state to a place where he knew he could find Black people gathered for their weekly shopping. He was armed with an AR-15-style military assault rifle and military-grade body armor. He wore a mounted camera on his helmet to livestream what was to come.

The racist assassin shot four people in the parking lot, killing three. He entered the store and shot down eight more people, killing six. As he violently ended the lives of people who ranged from a thirty-two-year-old sister to an eighty-two-year-old grandmother, he yelled out racial slurs while he shot them down. Salter shot and fired at the attacker, but his bullets bounced off the body armor. Then the attacker shot and killed the guard from Lockport. All ten of the victims who died were Black.

In the aftermath of the shooting a parade of political leaders came to Buffalo to visit the site of the killings and express their support for the community and the victims. This included President Joe Biden and First Lady Jill Biden, Vice President Kamala Harris, and New York Governor Kathy Hochul. In his statements at the grocery store turned memorial, Biden called racism "a poison running through our body politic."

Lockport marked the racist killings, one that took the life of a neighbor, in an unplanned way. By coincidence the following Monday evening a public forum had been scheduled by leaders of the school district's new My Brother's Keeper project. The purpose was to report on the project's activities and get people from the community more involved. It was held in the Common Council chambers at City Hall, the same room that had become the site of an unplanned community meeting with city leaders in the days after Troy Hodge's killing.

Once more the chambers become the site of an unscheduled community forum about the killing of a Black man from Lockport, and about the deep pain of racism and its impact on an entire community. Dr. Anna Barrett, who had been my daughter's Spanish teacher at Lockport High School, was leading the meeting. She was one of the few Black teachers in the district and understood the moment. Barret sidelined the regular agenda and instead turned the meeting into an impromptu community conversation about the tragedy the weekend before in Buffalo. I sat in the second row and listened.

Anguished people spoke of what it meant to feel like you and your family were being hunted. Some who spoke were in tears. It was clear how the shooting meant something entirely different if you were Black. Having Aaron Salter Jr. among the victims made it even more direct for people here. Many had known him, including the pastor, Mark Sanders, who told the group, "He was a quiet and unassuming man."

Anna Barrett, struggling to hold back her anger, read aloud from an emotional email she had received from Javeon Tomlinson, a former student of hers who has been a classmate of Salter's son all through school. The grief-stricken email read:

> What happened over the weekend is beyond EVIL. I feel for the people and their families. Nobody wakes up knowing this will be their last day here. What makes it worse is that all of the people were involved in the community! Deacons of churches and police officers etc. I grew up with Aaron Salter in elementary, middle and high school and I feel really bad. His dad was retired and just working in his spare time. It's not fair. The government talks about terrorism. What about the terrorism in America? Another press conference isn't enough and it's getting old, something needs to be done. It's 2022 still shooting us down like dogs in the street.

Beyond the impromptu forum in City Hall the Tops killings had other local implications. Our congressman at the time was Chris Jacobs, a conservative Republican in his forties serving his first term in a solidly Republican district where he could expect reelection without serious challenge for as long as he wanted to stay in Washington. He had all the trappings of a long House career ahead of him.

In the aftermath of the attack, Jacobs shocked everyone by announcing that he would break GOP ranks and support a federal ban on military assault weapons like the one used in Buffalo, along with high-capacity magazines. He announced, "I can't in good conscience sit back and say I didn't try to do something." A week later his once-promising political career was over.[6]

Despite being a longtime supporter of gun rights and the Second Amendment, his straying from a hardline position on assault weapons brought the wrath of gun rights groups and fellow Republicans. Other New York Republican House members denounced him, as did Donald Trump. The NRA called for his political head. A local gun rights group posted his cellphone number on the internet. Seven days after he had made his announcement on guns, Jacobs made another one: that he was dropping his bid for reelection that fall. "Look, if you're not going to take a stand on something like this, I don't know what you're going to take a stand on," Jacobs said, adding, "If you stray from a party position, you are annihilated."

Once more, in many ways at once, a larger national story, this one about racism and violence, could be seen close-up in one small community.

Through Tragedy a Community Finds a Clearer Voice

On June 16, 2020, Lockport marked the first anniversary of the death of Troy Hodge. Despite the arrival of the COVID-19 pandemic and its social distancing, more than a hundred people gathered at the home of Fatima Hodge and the driveway where her son had been killed by police twelve months before. The marking of the date took on a much larger national meaning as well, coming just three weeks after the police murder of George Floyd in Minneapolis, a Black man suffocated to death under the grinding knee of a uniformed officer.

As Lockport still awaited the results of the New York attorney general's investigation into Hodge's killing, a spirited and multiracial crowd gathered at the Hodge home and then marched the short distance to City Hall carrying homemade signs: I CAN'T BREATHE! SAY THEIR NAMES! BLACK LIVES

MATTER! That afternoon Lockport looked like many other communities that week around the country marching for racial justice. But it was an extraordinary sight in Lockport and was the lead story on the next day's front page of the *Union-Sun & Journal* in a poignant article by Connor Hoffman:[7]

> Hodge's mother, Fatima Hodge, who took part in the ceremony, spoke to the crowd and described her son as a man who loved to cook, go fishing and to "treat everybody right." She encouraged young people in attendance to take advantage of their chance to bring about positive changes in Lockport and surrounding communities.
>
> "There is a time and a place and a season for a change . . . I'm telling you this is the time. Nothing comes easy, but you got a choice to make that change," Hodge said.

After the march from the Hodge home arrived at City Hall, in a dramatic moment, marchers took a symbolic knee. Then the mayor, several local officials, and even the chief of police and some officers did the same.

In March 2021, nearly two years following Hodge's death, New York Attorney General Leticia James issued her office's report on its investigation of his death. The report concluded that there was insufficient evidence to establish that a crime had been committed by any of the police officers involved. In a statement the attorney general said: "I extend my deepest condolences to the family and loved ones of Troy Hodge. We engaged in an extensive and complete review of the facts in this case and determined that there was not sufficient evidence to prove that a crime had been committed."[8] No officers would be prosecuted. The attorney general did call on the Lockport Police Department and the Niagara County Sheriff to institute a set of reforms in how they handle such incidents; local officials, including Mayor Roman and the city's police board, used the report to push for those reforms. The Hodge family's attorney, Joseph Morath, made it clear that the Hodge family was frustrated and angry at the lack of prosecution. "We believe they should have been charged criminally for killing Troy." Meanwhile, internal disciplinary proceedings against the four officers involved, who had been assigned to desk duties in the aftermath of Hodge's death, just got bogged down in back-and-forth legal battles.

A few months after the attorney general report, a member of the Lockport Common Council, Mark Devine, put forward a resolution to end the city's disciplinary efforts against the officers involved, arguing that they had been exonerated. The move prompted a fierce response from the city's Black community at the council's hearing on the issue. They brought with them a giant photograph of Hodge, dead and carrying the dark bruises of his handling by the police.

One of those who spoke was his cousin, Ron Cheatham. "Do any of you guys understand what's at stake here? This is seriously uncalled for. Did any one of you come to Tina [Hodge's mother] and say, 'You know what, I'm sorry about your loss?' Did any one of you even care about what she has to go through every single day? I feel the pain. She's my cousin! She's crying all the time! Sometimes you can't even help her deal with it. And you're up here worrying about a resolution where a person already has a job? And you're worrying about him getting away from a desk? Are you serious? This is uncalled for! Did any of the officers come to Tina and say I'm sorry? It was an accident? Nobody apologized, not one of you!"

Hodge's mother, who had always been so composed in her public comments, was now finally driven to anger. "They beat my child like they beat a piece of steak," Hodge said. "They beat him like he was nothing!" Devine withdrew the resolution.

The following January, Niagara County Sheriff Michael Filicetti announced that he was hiring one of the Lockport police officers involved in Hodge's death, Marissa Bonito, to be a deputy in his department. He claimed that the attorney general report had exonerated her. Filicetti told the *Union-Sun & Journal* regarding Hodge's killing, "It was a tragic event, I will say that. I wouldn't have hired her if I wasn't confident she'd be a good deputy sheriff."

In December 2022 it was disclosed that Lockport had reached a $3 million settlement with the Hodge family, stemming from its wrongful death suit against the city. The award was paid for under a city insurance policy. The settlement with the family also required Lockport to commit to a package of police reforms. These included mandatory body-cam use as well as training in racial bias, deescalation, and how to manage people in mental distress. The agreement also required the Lockport Police Department to make an accelerated effort to recruit and hire minority police officers.

In the five years since I got my first lesson about race in Lockport from a little boy warning me about a police car, those issues have risen dramatically in the public eye. The tragedy of the death of a Black man in police hands had made racial issues in the city undeniable. The racial blindness, or worse, among leaders of the Lockport School District had come out into the open. The Black community and its allies had also begun to speak with a new and more powerful voice.

People crowded into school board meetings and held the district accountable. People held community forums on racial issues and created a public conversation. People demanded reforms from the police. A school was renamed for a powerful figure in Black city history. Two Black Lockportians were elected to the board of education. The school district hired its first African American superintendent.

Genuine racial justice is still a long way off in Lockport. Black students in the school district are still more than twice as likely to get suspended than White students. There is still not a single African American serving in either the city police or fire department, nor a single African American man teaching in the city's schools (and only a few Black women). Cheatham lost her bid for reelection to the school board in an election in which the old guard at the teachers' union threw its weight behind a slate of three White men.

Old and outdated attitudes about race are still not hard to find. A friend of mine here who ran for city alderman told me about his encounter with a local voter as he was knocking on doors. "What are you going to do about the Blacks?" a voter asked him. "They are asking for too much." Black members of the community say they still endure staring, epithets, and judgment as they live their lives in a mostly White community.

In Lockport, as elsewhere, issues about race make people feel uncomfortable. They are pushed under the table or ignored entirely. But they do not disappear. Sometimes that racism is overt. Other times it is baked into the ways that important institutions do business. I can see now why that young boy on that summer afternoon after we first arrived warned me in the way he did.

Chapter Four

A Rebellion against Renewable Power

The Niagara County Fair is held for a week in late July and early August just on the outskirts of Lockport. It is a centerpiece of the local summer. The fair comes complete with three large, open-air pavilions of animals displayed by the county's young 4-H Club members. Here you can see eight-year-olds showing off their prized rabbits. You can see teenagers compete for ribbons with their cows, hogs, and goats. The long row of food vendors serves up a whole assortment of local favorites, from hot Italian sausages to deep-fried Snickers bars. The midway includes a variety of twisty, swirly rides that make children scream and make me sick to my stomach. There are different shows that offer a magician doing magic, dogs doing jumping tricks, and my favorite: a woman in a silver-sequined leotard who can hang from a long rope using nothing more than her teeth.

Off to one side and less visited is the pavilion where the people with something to sell set up shop. During our family's first trip to the fair in the summer of 2017, as we walked through the sellers' building I was asked by well-meaning people at small booths if I was satisfied with my car insurance, whether my rain gutters needed cleaning, or if I might be in need of new windows. I managed to skirt by them all without getting sucked in, even though it meant forgoing several free keychains and pens.

Then I ran into a booth with a small banner that read: STOP INDUSTRIAL WIND.

Against the Wind

'Who opposes wind power?' I thought to myself. My curiosity led me to the booth where I expected to meet some sort of antiwind zealot with a half-baked argument and tales of a government conspiracy. Instead, I met Pam Atwater.

Pam, I would learn later, is a trained electrical engineer who worked for IBM years ago. At their home on the rural shore of Lake Ontario, she and her husband Randy have solar panels on their barns' rooftops and a geothermal heating system under the ground. As the president of the local school board, Randy championed a project that installed eighteen hundred solar panels on school property. In short, this was not a family of climate change deniers, puppets of the fossil fuel industry, or adversaries of the national transition to clean energy. Pam Atwater, however, was the most visible leader in a community uprising against a giant wind energy project being pushed for development along the lakeshore.

The Atwaters live in the tiny town of Somerset (pop. 2,662), a sweet patch of rural life right along the southern edge of the smallest of the five Great Lakes. It is the same farming community where Lynn and I took our granddaughter, Isabella, when she was two years old to a u-pick blueberry farm. She may have broken all records for the amount of blueberries any single human being has ever put in her mouth at one time. On a clear day from the lakeshore you can see across to the distant skyline of Toronto, but here urban life seemed like it might as well exist on another planet.

The gem of this part of Niagara County is the tiny hamlet of Olcott (pop. 1,155) and its children's amusement park. The park was originally opened in 1898 and during its heyday through the 1920s it was like a miniature Coney Island for tourists from across New York. After years of later neglect the park was brought back to life in 2002 by a dedicated volunteer effort by the people of the town. In summers today small crowds of visitors from both near and far come to enjoy the village's beautiful restored rides. These include a vintage carousel and an assortment of slowly rotating boats, cars, and planes sized just right for small children (like our granddaughters). And at a very old-fashioned price of twenty-five cents per ride, the town has made it possible for an entire family to pass a whole happy afternoon for five dollars.

There are good reasons that the people who live along this lakeshore love it exactly as it is.

Pam Atwater was and remains one of the leaders of Save Ontario Shores (SOS), a community organization waging a fierce and well-orchestrated campaign to stop a project called Lighthouse Wind, being pushed by a Virginia-based corporation, Apex Clean Energy. Apex boasts in its public relations material that it "was founded with a singular focus: to accelerate the shift to clean energy."[1]

On the shores of Lake Ontario that shift involved a plan to construct as many as seventy industrial wind turbines, each of which would be taller than the Washington Monument. The huge turbines would be taller than any buildings in New York State outside of New York City, taller than the tallest buildings in Buffalo and Rochester, according to SOS.[2] In the eyes of many who occupy the pastoral lands along the lake, the project seemed like an invasion of monster aliens right out of a science fiction movie.

The community members involved in SOS did their homework and laid out a whole set of substantial concerns about what the turbines would mean for the local environment.[3] They said that the giant turbines would cause havoc with the light of day by sending flickering shadows across the land and cause havoc with the dark rural night sky by filling it with bright red tower lights. The turbines would cause noise pollution and enormous local disruption during construction. They also said that the towers would interfere with one of the most important bird migration corridors in North America. If none of these arguments won over local neighbors, I suspect what did was warnings about the about the potential negative impact on local home values.

The community effort against the wind turbines began in 2015 and lasted years. It included surveys of local residents, volumes of careful research, methodic intervention in the state siting process, a stream of articles and op-eds, testimony and lobbying aimed at state and local officials, letter-writing campaigns, going toe-to-toe with the company on every detail of the project, and even a special Mother's Day campaign.[4] As a model of grassroots organizing the effort was deadly serious and ticked off all the boxes of smart activism. By 2022 it looked like their efforts had succeeded, temporarily at least, with an announcement by the company that it was withdrawing its state permit application.

A few weeks after my visit to the county fair and encounter with Pam Atwater, I made a road trip across New York State to rural western Connecticut to reunite with friends there. One of them is a well-known climate activist who has been writing widely read books and magazine articles on the subject for many years. He lives year round in a cabin in a beautiful forest unlikely to ever be touched by any large-scale solar or wind project. I told him about my chance meeting with the opponents of an industrial-scale wind project and confessed that I thought there was legitimacy to their concerns.

"We are in the middle of a planetary emergency," he told me. "They are just going to have to suck it up." I had been back in the US from Bolivia for less than a month and realized that the politics of moving to clean energy here were going to be a lot more complicated than I thought.

Big Energy Goals Dictated from Elsewhere

New York State has no shortage of ambition when it comes to its renewable energy goals. In 2019, as part of the global effort to address catastrophic climate change, New York adopted some of the boldest renewable energy goals in the nation. By 2030 the state aims to generate 70 percent of all its electricity from hydropower, wind and solar, an increase of more than double in less than a decade. It aims to generate 100 percent of its electricity from renewables by 2040. No other US state has a target that aims higher or faster. The architects of the plan have called it "a comprehensive roadmap to build a clean, resilient, and affordable energy system for all New Yorkers."[5]

That plan was largely driven by climate and environmental activists in New York City. One of the things that I learned quickly here is that for many Western New Yorkers that city of nearly nine million people a day's drive away might as well be in another country. Many people here would sever that common statehood in a heartbeat if they could. I also learned that the political activists and politicians in the city had no hesitancy about using their clout in state government to impose their political agendas onto their distant rural neighbors. Resentment against that runs high here.

New York City currently generates just 3 percent of the electricity it uses from energy sources that do not produce greenhouse gasses. This became even more the case after the achievement of another recent goal of environmental activists, the closure of the Indian Point nuclear power plant in 2021. The city isn't expected to increase its local production of renewable energy by much anytime soon.[6] This means that to meet the state's ambitious renewable energy goals all that renewable power will need to be generated elsewhere. In New York State that elsewhere is upstate and the far west, including here in Niagara County.

As many locals will quickly tell you, Niagara County already generates far more electrical power than it uses, thanks to two immense electricity-generating plants operating at Niagara Falls. Those plants use the power of the Falls to generate enough electricity to power 3.8 million homes. Just over half that is generated on the US side of the Falls.[7] Niagara County has fewer than a hundred thousand homes. This means that more than 90 percent of all that power goes elsewhere.

The presence of the Falls also makes Niagara County a magnet for industrial-scale wind and solar power projects for another reason. As one renewable energy developer explained to me, Niagara County possesses the three ingredients that wind and solar corporations need most: open land, landowners willing to lease it, and close access to high-capacity power transmission cables, with the third being the most key. High-capacity cables like that already crisscross the county to export electricity from the Falls.

Connecting large-scale wind and solar projects to big cables like these is called "wheeling." The more of it that companies have to do the less economically viable projects become. In many parts of Niagara County, because of the high transmission cables already in place, they don't have to do that wheeling very far.

But in the eyes of many people in this part of New York, the state's ambitious climate plan looks not so much like a transition to cleaner power as it does a plot to use Niagara County's farms, shores, and open fields as a way to keep the lights on in Times Square.

Solar Battles

On a cold autumn evening in November 2019, more than two hundred people crowded into the volunteer fire department meeting hall in rural Gasport, a twenty-minute drive east of Lockport. It was the first time I had seen a parking lot full of so many pickups. I went to the meeting at the urging of a woman named Margaret Darroch and her daughter Jeanna Marie. I knew the two of them from Lockport's Saturday Community Market. Their family owns and operates the small Stone Hollow Farm and baking business. Our conversations about solar power projects began over my return visits to their booth to buy some of the best-tasting scones on Earth.

Margaret was a member of the Hartland Town Planning Board. In this part of Western New York, public entities called towns and villages overlap and intertwine in ways that are nearly impossible to understand. But the planning board was where the issue of building solar fields had landed, and Margaret was concerned. She was especially worried about a proposed industrial-scale solar project called Ridge View Solar. It is a mammoth project that aims to erect solar panels across a total of two thousand acres of local farmland.

The Ridge View Solar project was the topic of the night in the fire hall. The meeting began with the Pledge of Allegiance and a Christian prayer and then turned to the speaker for the evening, a man named Charlie Fendt. Fendt is a self-described "emergency management consultant" from Rochester. His biography drew generously on the fact that he had once taken a set of management and planning courses offered by the Federal Emergency Management Administration (FEMA). By the time that got translated into his self-introduction it made it sound as if he actually worked for the federal agency that dealt with hurricanes, earthquakes, and wildfires. For months he had been traveling around to community meetings like this one all across Western New York like an itinerant preacher. His sermon was about the lethal perils of solar power.

He told his rapt listeners that the electrical storage batteries required on large solar fields carried the explosive risks of a large bomb. He said that terrorists might even strike the batteries with attack drones to set them off. If the panels caught fire, he warned, they would release dangerous toxic fumes into the air that would spread for miles. He also told worried farmers that the same hailstorms capable of shredding a crop of apples in minutes could also pummel the glass panels into broken shards that would leave the land unplantable far into the future.

It didn't matter that his wild claims didn't line up with the facts. For a community debating a huge and unfamiliar solar project these charges only further inflamed local doubts.

In Niagara County, solar energy projects come in various different sizes. At the small end sit projects like the one on my roof in Lockport. I'm quite proud of the fourteen solar panels that sit staring at the sky on the rear side of our family's house. We had them installed in 2019 and have been generating more electricity than we use every year since.

As I began writing about solar power in my columns in the *Union-Sun & Journal* I enjoyed telling readers that I had a solar-powered washer and dryer in my basement. Through people's questions I also began to understand some of the common misconceptions about how solar power systems operate.

People asked if I had to have a giant solar battery in my garage? I explained that I did not, that all the power generated from my roof is exported into the larger grid, like making a deposit in a bank. People asked if I still had power on cloudy days and during Western New York's long, cold, gray winters. I explained that all that extra electricity that my roof generates in spring, summer, and fall gets credited back to me as our house uses energy from the grid in winter. As questions like these get asked and answered, and as people tune in to the economic benefits of state and federal tax breaks and big savings on energy bills, more families are making the transition. In 2023 just over six hundred homes across the county had gone solar with the numbers steadily rising.

But the misconceptions about solar, and the legitimate concerns, get a lot bigger when it comes to systems bigger than one on a house rooftop. That played out in a very public way in a heated local battle over one small farming family's decision to add solar power to the mix of what it wanted to produce.

Tina and Karl Kowalski are the fifth generation to operate their family's Maverick Farm. It sits at the intersection of two well-traveled roads in the Town of Lockport (the Town is a separate entity from the City of Lockport, right next door). It also sits just down the street from the popular Lockport Nature Trail where I walk our dog Lola several mornings a week. The Kowalskis' farm specializes in certified organic dairy products and operates a small herd of cattle. The family links its environmental values to its devout Christian faith. The farm's website quotes from Genesis and declares, "We believe that this land is only on loan to us from our Heavenly Father and we are to have dominion over the land for the crops we grow and the animals we raise."

Small farms like theirs are increasingly difficult to keep economically sustainable. They are squeezed by rising costs on the one hand and competition from large-scale farms on the other. The solution for many is diversification, to become less reliant on any one crop that might suddenly hit a year of turbulence from rough weather or economics. In early 2021 the Kowalskis sought to diversify in a direction that surprised most of their neighbors when it became public. They were seeking permits to lease forty-six acres of their land to a solar developer to erect a field of solar panels.

Reaction was swift. Almost overnight the roads all around the farm were crowded with new black, white, and red signs proclaiming, No Solar! Town officials began holding a series of community forums on the proposed project and those meetings were packed. One of the most vocal opponents was a neighbor across the street from the farm, Brent Powley. In typical small-town fashion, Powley had also been the DJ at my daughter's wedding six years before. "One bee isn't going to hurt you, but the hive's going to sting you and the hive is coming," he told the *Union-Sun & Journal,* linking the Kowalskis' proposed small project to the far larger ones being proposed for elsewhere in the county.[8]

Another vocal opponent was Barbara Outten, owner of McCollum Farms, which sits just adjacent to the Kowalski's farm. With three thousand head of cattle it is one of the largest farms in the area. Interviewed for the newspaper, she repeated the same warnings launched by Fendt at the fire hall forum. This included warnings about hazardous smoke that she said could kill off parts of her herd if the solar field ever caught fire. "If I was a politician and represented the constituents of this area and they didn't want it, it's a no brainer what I would do—give us back our life and our liberty and the pursuit of what's best for our community and our children," she said.

It was also clear, however, that the real objections held by most people were simply that people didn't want to look at a field of solar panels. At the town forum I attended neighbors spoke about having moved out to the green countryside and built homes there specifically to get away from the concrete, steel, and other mainstays of the city. As Powley said, "They used to look out their windows at beautiful, open fields, Now they'll be looking this huge silver landscape."

The community pressure on the Kowalskis to drop the project was intense. During the heat of the tension over the project, Dale McCollum, another owner of McCollum Farms, sprayed pesticides on nearly an acre of the Kowalskis' land. It was a move that took that land out of organic production for at least three years. Karl Kowalski told the newspaper afterward that he confronted his neighbor over the spraying, "I said, 'This is harassment!' and he said, 'Your solar is harassment!'"

Despite the pressure from their neighbors, the Kowalskis insisted that the solar field was key to keeping the farm going for another generation. Tina Kowalski told the newspaper, "Farming is our passion and something we cannot imagine not doing. Installing the solar will allow us to be able to continue farming. We wish for our neighbors to understand that we are not doing this to upset them, but instead are doing it for us, to enable us to keep doing what we love. It will just look different than it has in the past."[9]

Town officials were caught in exactly the kind of bind that local officials like least. On the one hand, the solar developer involved, California-based

Renewable Properties, had complied with all the requirements of the Town's solar law. This included, as the company repeated at every opportunity, spending a large sum of money on required environmental studies. On the other hand, public opinion seemed to be settling pretty hard in opposition, at least the most vocal part. The company also didn't do itself any favors by sending out spokespeople from San Francisco who spoke in technobabble and who dodged questions about what exactly would happen to all the panels after their use was over.

Lockport's Town Board tried to split the baby in half by voting for a temporary moratorium on all new solar development, which they hoped would calm down the neighbors without drawing a lawsuit from Renewable Properties. But the company made it clear in public that blocking the project would be a serious violation of the Town's own rules. I presumed that in private the threat of legal action was more direct.

The moratorium was soon amended to exclude the project at Maverick Farms. Construction began in early 2023. The field went operational in 2024, hardly visible from the street adjacent to it. All but a few of the angry signs disappeared. Meanwhile, while neighbors in the Town of Lockport were focusing their attention on a battle against solar panels on forty-five acres of a family farm, a much bigger fight was brewing just up the road. This one was over the third category of solar projects, the full-on industrial scale variety. This included two specific projects that cover farmland fifty times that of the field on the Kowalski farm.

When Solar Goes Massive Scale

It doesn't take much looking at the well-polished promotional materials for EDF Renewables to spot the standard trappings of a modern megacorporation. You have the big buzzword slogans: "Creativity. Ambition. Imagination." You have the proud boasts: "Leading the renewable energy charge for 35 years and counting." You have the nods to being good corporate citizens: "What helps to define us is our commitment to the communities in which we operate. At the core of every EDF project is sustainability and corporate social responsibility."

In the middle of 2019, EDF announced plans for a two-thousand-acre solar field project spread across the eastern Niagara County community of Hartland. If completed, the project would cover the equivalent of more than fifteen hundred NFL football fields worth of farmland with glass and steel solar panels. It would be one of the largest solar installations in the US. The company proudly proclaimed that "the Project will safely generate enough clean, renewable electricity to power 90,000 New York households."

EDF planned to stitch together that mass of acreage with a web of leasing agreements with farmers across the communities—most of them with large landholdings for cattle. One of the largest of those owners told me he had signed an agreement to lease 350 acres to EDF for the solar project. At the going rate for leases, that would mean some $350,000 per year in payments from the company every year for at least twenty-five years. The stakes involved were huge. But even some of the less giant farms saw an important opportunity.

Becker Farms is a beautiful 340-acre family farm in Gasport (the same community where the fire hall meeting was held). It was founded in 1894 and today it offers everything from pick-your-own apples in the fall, to a venue for weddings, to a small pub where my family goes to hear local musicians. Mindy Vizcarra, a great-granddaughter of the founders, owns the farm with her husband Oscar. The two are supporters of the Ridge View Solar project, and their farm is one of those slated to have a solar field built on its open land. Mindy explained to me that a fifty-acre plot of her farm, which she currently rents out for $80 an acre per year to someone who grows grass for hay, would be leased instead for $1,000 an acre per year for the solar project. She says the solar panels would be in the middle of her land, closed off behind a chain-link fence and shielded from view by trees, bushes, and a berm.

Because the full project would be spread out across many farms, Mindy told me, "It's not really as much land as you think. It's not going to change things as much as people think it's going to change things." In Becker Farms' case, she said, the area around the solar panels would be planted with native wildflowers to create new pollinating lands for the threatened bee population. Mindy told me that she sees the project both as a way to further diversify her farm's sources of income and as an opportunity to contribute to a cleaner energy future: "We are taking a stand and being a part of the solution."

But as news of the large-scale project spread, so did the apprehensions. Several miles east of Becker farms, on the other side of Hartland, is Margaret Darroch's small Stone Hollow Farm with her animals, produce, and thriving small bakery. She says that her hesitations about Ridge View began with what she says were serious misrepresentations by the company to the community. "They told us that it was just 10 percent of our agricultural land. It's 27 percent of our agricultural land," she said. "Nobody is against solar. It's the size."

Margaret says that the huge project, which would involve two years of heavy construction, would have a major impact on the land that this part of the state relies on for its agriculture. "You can't just drive big equipment and put up concrete blocks on top of soil and have it be okay," she said. "To take such a rich area and use it for this purpose makes no sense to me."

Others objecting to the project noted that the fields of panels would be spread out across a wide area, necessitating a giant web of connecting power cables linking them to power stations and the electrical grid. Those heavy cables would also have to crisscross local farmland.

The project's manager, Kevin Campbell, came to EDF Renewables after a long stint running field operations for Shell Oil in Canada. The company's pitch to the community was wrapped in the language of money. It promised that the project would generate more than $1.5 million per year in new revenue to the local communities, as much as $1,000 per household, it said. The project pledged that it would pay $2.5 million per year to participating landowners.[10] Those were big numbers in small towns and enough to win the project some influential supporters alongside the increasingly vocal opponents.

Not far to the west, in the Town of Cambria, another industrial solar company, Cypress Creek Renewables, was pushing for development of a second large-scale solar field, the nine-hundred-acre Bear Ridge Project. There the corporation not only spoke the language of landowner profit and local government revenue but of climate change as well. Company officials said that the project would generate enough clean, renewable electricity to power between 15,000 and 20,000 single-family homes and that it would offset an estimated 160,000 tons of carbon dioxide annually: the equivalent of removing 15,000 cars from the road each year.[11]

Both projects eventually sparked widespread community opposition, some of it more fact-based than others. One night in 2021 I went to a community meeting in Cambria where opponents of the Bear Ridge Project were gathered to hear an update. The town supervisor (the equivalent of town mayor), a bespectacled older fellow named Wright Ellis, warned the crowded fire hall that a solar battery array in California had recently exploded, "with a blast radius of more than two miles." The fears of what a similar system could mean in their small farming community only became deeper.

Afterward I looked into the claim and found that the facts didn't exactly align with how he explained it. The incident involved was not in

California but at a solar installation in McMicken, Arizona. In 2015 a storage battery in a trailer full of them shorted out, overheated, and released flammable gases inside. Local firefighters did not understand that the safety protocol was to let the gasses burn out in the sealed container and not to open it. When they did, the gasses caught a spark and exploded. Nine firefighters and police were injured. The reach of the blast was essentially the length of the parking lot, not two miles.[12]

Solar batteries have indeed suffered issues with fire and potentially toxic fumes, including a widely reported case in New York State in 2023.[13] But the inflated tale told by the town supervisor that night was indicative of the kind of misinformation that was tossed into the mix of local debate about solar power expansion in the county. Instead of discussing issues such as the environmental impacts on farmland and whether leasing for solar would freeze out farmers seeking land to lease, communities were fretting over giant battery explosions that never happened. Instead of asking hard questions about whether the companies were getting backroom deals to escape fair local taxation, opponents were making up tales of shattered glass from hail strikes.

A deeply important community issue was getting stuck between the slick public relations claims of the companies on the one hand and wild declarations by some of those who took the lead in opposing them.

The Niagara County Solar Study Group

In 2020 I approached Joyce Miles at the newspaper with the idea of writing a series on solar issues. She agreed and the result was a three-part series titled "Knowledge and Power" that ran that November.

I wrote about Charlie Fendt and other tellers of tall tales designed to frighten people. I quoted Mindy Vizcarra who touted the benefit to local farmers and Margaret Darroch who worried about the long-term impact of taking farmland out of commission. I asked the project manager for the Ridge View Solar project, Kevin Campbell, why the company wanted to site the project on agricultural land instead of on some of the contaminated brownfields in Niagara County. Campbell told me they hadn't looked into it.

I also wrote about the financial deals that some very large corporations were cutting with local governments in which they would make special payments in lieu of normal property taxes (known as PILOTs). Local officials in support of these deals were quick to argue that without them the solar companies would just move elsewhere and the cities and towns involved would just end up with nothing. Looking at the numbers for a forty-seven-acre solar project being proposed in the City of Lockport I wrote, "The City's annual revenue from the project would come to about $12,000, roughly the cost of putting on the city's annual July 4th fireworks show. The annual property tax break that the company wants would be more than $87,000. That's on top of the state and federal subsidies it would receive, worth roughly $5 million, nearly half the cost of building it."

Despite the intense interest that solar projects seemed to be generating around the county, there didn't seem to be much interest in getting into the weeds of the issues involved. The people who were most vocal about solar development, on both sides, seemed less interested in facts I presented than in debating what side I was on.

Provoking a deeper debate was going to require some help. To get it I reached out to a diverse group of people around the county, with different backgrounds and different perspectives on solar power. Together we hoped that our diversity of voices, and shared commitment to get the facts, might have more impact. Thus was born the Niagara County Solar Study Group.

Two of the people who joined had been quite public about their solar concerns. This included Margaret Darroch, the small farmer and member of the Hartland Town Planning Board, and Richard Brown, a retired NY Supreme Court clerk who had spoken out publicly against the solar project proposed in the City of Lockport down the street from his home. We also had two people with well-established environmental credentials. This included Jessica Glaser, a health systems professional who served on the Town of Pendleton Conservation Advisory Council, and Zuzanna Drozdz, a Lockport-based landscape designer and adjunct faculty in the University of Buffalo Architecture Department.

To bring in the agricultural perspective we had Jim Bittner, the owner of a large fruit farm out near the lake and a longtime leader in several county and statewide agricultural organizations. He told us at our first meeting, "It is good to be a part of something that is actually looking at the facts." We also had Randy Atwater, recently retired from management in fruit processing and who served as president of the school board for the small lakeshore communities of the Barker Central School District (and the husband of Pam Atwater who had led opposition to the Lighthouse Wind project).

We began with ambitious plans for what to research and how to get what we learned out into the community. We tried to do this amidst the challenge of a global pandemic. Our meetings in person ended but the combination of winter nights and Zoom lent itself well to a set of interviews with energy experts and various state officials who helped us get to the complexities of solar siting in Western New York, and there were plenty of complexities to deal with.

By spring we had more information than we knew what to do with. Randy made a wise suggestion: publish a new series in the two county dailies, the *Union-Sun & Journal* and the *Niagara Gazette*, that would go much deeper than my original series the year before. The editors of both newspapers were game and at the end of April 2022 they published our five-part series, "Solar Know How."

Randy's introductory article, "6,000 Acres and Counting" summarized the complicated array of solar projects being proposed around the county, from small to enormous. It also explained how New York State had recently taken the siting powers over the largest projects out of the hands of local communities and turned it over to a new state agency, the Office of Renewable Energy Siting (ORES). That shifting of power to the state had become a point of fierce resentment in local communities across Western New York. State officials argued that if every small town could scuttle industrial-scale solar projects because they didn't like them, New York could never meet its renewable energy goals. Local communities saw it as a giant power grab by New York City environmentalists content to pave over farmland with glass and steel.

Our next two articles, also by Randy, looked specifically at the impact of solar development on farming and agriculture. He explained the two sides of the coin:

> Good farmland is typically flat and farm fields are often quite large, making for relatively quick and easy installation of large-scale solar projects. Solar development can also supplement farm income and thereby may help keep some farms in business.
>
> On the other hand, using farmland for solar development will remove it from agricultural production for 25 years or more, with a range of impacts. Land lost to solar development will likely reduce the amount of farmland available for farmers to rent, raising costs substantially.

That loss of land available to farmers to rent is a serious concern. Young people eager to get into farming often start out by renting land as a way of building a business and setting themselves up to buy land later. Cutting off that onramp by using rented land for solar fields can potentially have a huge impact on keeping small farming alive for another generation.

We also wrote about the potential of siting solar projects on "brownfields," parcels of land left contaminated by old factories and other polluters. Niagara County, home to the infamous Love Canal toxic waste site, sadly, has plenty of them.

We looked at the growing effort to use land for solar panels and agricultural uses at the same time: "Some current solar farms graze sheep or raise chickens or geese to keep grass levels down. Growing shade tolerant crops such as tomatoes, potatoes, spinach, lettuce, and raspberries under solar canopies has already been shown to be successful in Germany and the Netherlands. Some solar developers offer plans to plant wildflowers and other species that support local pollinators such as bees and butterflies, something also essential to parts of our local agriculture." Zuzanna, our landscape designer, wrote a column for the series about how solar projects could be designed to minimize environmental impacts:

> As communities consider proposed solar projects, there are some specific things that can be required to protect local wildlife and the local environment. Utility-scale solar facilities are required to install fencing that is at least 7 feet high. This could have the effect of blocking huge amounts of acreage from the wildlife populations that use that land. Installing wildlife-permeable fencing that allows raccoons, rabbits and other small critters, and underplanting the solar panels with native vegetation, can make these same facilities "solar sanctuaries."

I wrote the last piece in the series, once more returning to "the money part" of solar projects:

> It is standard practice (including here in Niagara County) for solar developers to seek to avoid local tax payments altogether and instead negotiate a Payment in Lieu of Taxes (PILOT). These are side deals that are always for far less than what a normal tax would be and far less than the local tax bills paid by other businesses.
>
> But taxing private projects is not the only way for local communities to derive economic benefit from solar development.

Another option is for cities, towns, and school districts to actually own their own solar projects. One example, here in Niagara County, is a new solar array being constructed by the Barker School District. The system will pay for itself in approximately 15 years and then produce free electricity for the district for at least another decade after that, saving the Barker schools an estimated $1.4 million.

Our article series offered our communities and local officials a deep dive into a set of issues that had been mired for years in common misunderstandings and wild assertions. It came from neither a "solar is great" or "solar is evil" perspective. It challenged the assertions and moves of some of the large corporations involved and also combatted some of the hyperbole of solar adversaries.

The series was widely read, especially among the people most involved in solar development issues in the county. We heard from them afterward. This included owners of some of the large farms looking to lease their land for solar projects, solar developers, and members of the public who were following the issue. We also sent a complete copy of the series to all the members of the Niagara County Legislature.

But did all this have any actual impact? Our work was based on an assumption that amidst all of the emotional debate about solar development in our county that there would also be some hunger for real information. But what seemed to interest most people was not analysis but exaggerated tales of exploding solar batteries or the possibility of having their taxes lowered if their community took in new revenue.

In all of this I learned another small-town lesson. The way to engage people on an issue like solar is not with analysis of the bigger picture or the deeper issues. It was to weigh in on very specific, very local controversies of the moment, like the neighbors' fight over solar at the Kowalksi Farm or how much our towns would get from specific projects. This was what I had done on the Lockport School District's facial recognition surveillance project with good success. In retrospect it would likely have been a more effective way to get the community engaged in the debate over solar projects as well.

Shuttering a Coal Plant

In January of 2016 the Sierra Club of New York announced to its members that it had scored what it called a "groundbreaking" victory. After years of activist pressure including demonstrations and rallies targeting state policymakers, Governor Andrew Cuomo had announced new regulations that would shut down the state's two last remaining coal-powered electrical plants. The Club wrote, "New York's governor hit the spot with environmental advocates when he promised in Wednesday's State of the State Address that New York will retire all of its coal plants by 2020." The Sierra Club's young Beyond Coal organizer, Daniel Sherrell, explained, "We've fundamentally changed the politics on coal in the State of New York."

One of those last two coal plants was the Kintigh Generating Station located in the small town of Somerset, seventeen miles north of Lockport on the shore of Lake Ontario. Opened in 1984, the plant is a local landmark. Its 625-foot-tall smokestack (demolished in January 2025) could be seen on a clear day from Toronto across the lake. It was built with a capacity to generate 675 megawatts of electricity per year (enough to power more than four hundred thousand homes). Coal was delivered to the plant via a small railroad spur from Lockport. The electricity produced from that coal was delivered into the Western New York power grid through some of the same heavy transmission cables that delivered hydro-electric power from Niagara Falls, helping keep the lights on across the region.

When the plant was running at full capacity it employed more than two hundred people. That is a very large number in a community with a population of just over twenty-five hundred. The wide-open lands around the plant are for farming, filled with groves of apple and cherry trees, summer corn, and blueberries. Regardless of whatever smoke and noise and other undesirable side effects it spat back at its neighbors, the Kintigh plant was both a keystone of the local economy and an accepted part of the community.

Under the new state regulations championed by the Sierra Club and other groups based hundreds of miles away, the plant was closed in March 2020. By the end, however, its operations were a shadow of what they had once been. The value of the plant as an electricity producer had been undercut by the rise of much cheaper power generated from plants fueled by natural gas. New York State has more than a dozen such facilities.[14] By the end, the plant in Somerset had become little more than a back-up operation to ensure that the New York grid maintained power if its other sources left a gap. In 2018 it only operated twenty-five days during the entire year.

The grand claims by Sierra Club organizers that the closure was "a critical step in moving New York away from fossil fuels" were not matched by the smallness of what was involved.

A Rebellion against Renewable Power | 91

For the community though, the plant's closure meant many things at once, all of them difficult. It meant the sudden loss of a key revenue source that helped pay for local schools and local services. It meant a wider economic blow to the community as a whole. A project of that size in a small community means a lot of money moving around to local stores and businesses.

Then there were the workers, forty-five of them at the time of the plant's closure.

"This plant is my life," Darlene Lutz, age sixty, told a reporter for the *New York Times* who came here to cover the closing. Lutz had been the only woman ever employed there in a senior operating position. John Mason, the plant's operation manager, told the newspaper, "I just worry about the guys who are in their 40s. Some of us are retiring, a few folks in their 20s are young enough to start over, but for those guys in the middle, it's tough." Several people I spoke with told me that it felt as if their community had been gutted.

For many it seemed that what downstate environmentalists were really celebrating was not some meaningful cut in carbon emissions. It seemed a lot more like the Sierra Club and the others were just interested in scoring a notch in their belt, a political win they could brag about to their activists and donors. Paul Schnell, a conservation activist and wildlife photographer who worked at the plant for three decades, wrote in the *Union-Sun & Journal* that the plant's closure "will likely find politicians and their 'green' allies fist bumping, shouting and high-fiving."[15] The plant's closure became yet another source of resentment for local communities about environmental policies created by people far away who seemed oblivious to the realities up close.

In 2016 when the Sierra Club heralded the announcement of the Kintigh Plant's closure, it was careful to add that it had also advocated for a "just transition for communities and workers." The just transition according to the Club included "worker retraining and transition funding for communities where fossil fuel plants have been permanently shut down."[16] But what did that really mean for the people along the lakeshore?

The Sierra Club's big plan was for the construction of those seventy giant wind turbines. The Club was a strong backer of the Apex corporation's project, calling it "environmentally sound."[17] Left out of the Club's reasoning were all the environmental complaints from the people who would actually have to live amidst the giant rotating turbines, and the fact that the project would generate virtually no permanent jobs to replace the ones that were lost. That did not seem like much of a just transition to the affected communities.

Scrambling to find some way to survive economically in the face of the plant's closure, community leaders listened to a different option being pitched by the plant's owner, Beowulf Energy. The company wanted to build and operate a giant data storage and processing center at the site of the old plant. It would come complete, they pledged, with a large array of solar panels on the old plant's grounds to help provide the needed power. The company also said that the data center would create as many as 160 permanent well-paid jobs. It was a sweet proposal (on paper), an old-school coal plant replaced with a modern data center processing things like people's Facebook posts, all run on sustainable power.

Even I got sucked in, for a moment. In July 2019 I wrote a column for the *Union-Sun & Journal* titled, "Somerset Deserves Support of Downstate Environmentalists."

> The push to close down the nation's coal plants is not without good reason. Coal is responsible for a third of the country's carbon emissions and is a leading contributor to global climate change. The abandonment of Somerset and its neighboring communities, however, is both unfair to those communities and bad politics for fighting climate change.
>
> The people of Somerset are not sitting around waiting for the environmentalist cavalry to arrive; they have a plan. They have a company ready to convert the plant into a high-tech data processing center. If New York climate change groups want to accelerate a transition to clean energy, they need communities like Somerset to be their allies not their adversaries. One way to do that is to make Somerset an example and offer serious support to its efforts to reinvent itself in a sustainable way.

A week later I received an email from Somerset's town supervisor, Dan Engert. In addition to running the small-town government he was also a Niagara County Deputy Sheriff. He asked if I would come out to a community rally in support of the data center and speak. The shoreline was one of the most politically conservative corners of the county. There were still Trump signs proudly displayed on many properties. Apparently, he thought having the county's token liberal columnist would be useful amid the collection of local Republican politicians lined up to speak.

It wasn't until I was on the drive out there on a sunny summer afternoon that I fully took in where I was going and asked myself the question: "You idiot, what in the hell have you gotten yourself into now?"

After I arrived at the large open field I wandered through the crowd introducing myself and was relieved that people seemed so friendly. Rarely had I felt more like an outsider. I figured I had some time to listen to what the other speakers had to say and come up with a message that would fit in. That was when Engert told me that they wanted me to speak first.

In a bit of a panic, I went for the blueberries story. After telling people (and meaning it) that they were lucky to live in one of the most beautiful places in the country, I talked about how Lynn and I had taken our two year old granddaughter, Bella, just the week before, down the road to Russell's U-Pick. I told them how I had witnessed a tiny human cramming more fresh blueberries in her mouth than I thought any living creature could. People laughed out loud. Everyone there had picked blueberries on that farm at one point or another. Most of them had probably done it with a child or grandchild. They could see exactly the scene I was talking about but with the children they loved. After that I went on to explain that it was because I had a grandchild that I was so concerned about climate change, but that communities like Somerset deserved to be supported through the transition.

That summer afternoon, in the shadow of a coal plant about to be shuttered, I learned one of the most valuable lessons about reaching across the great political divide. Start by talking about what you love in common. That afternoon, surrounded by people with an utterly different life experience and worldview than mine, I spoke genuinely about how much I loved and appreciated the beauty of their community and the joys that came with being a grandfather. It didn't matter if it made any converts. It opened a door that allowed people to listen.

In the meantime, that great solar-powered data center on the site of a former coal electricity plant turned out to be a giant Trojan horse.

In March 2022 the newly renamed TeraWulf Corporation announced the opening of its Lake Mariner Data Center on the site of the old Somerset coal plant. Its product, however, would not be something as benign as the cloud storage of people's photos of their grandchildren. The new center would be dedicated exclusively to data mining for cryptocurrency. Humanity, facing an existential crisis driven by how we use energy, had managed to invent a new form of invisible money that required massive amounts of electrical power. The good people and community of Somerset ended up on the front lines of helping it happen.

Terawulf's new data center has a target of five hundred megawatts of bitcoin mining, an enormous operation. That means five hundred megawatts of energy usage. The corporation pledged that 93 percent of the energy it uses would be carbon neutral. In classic corporate public relations speak it said, "This innovative project leverages existing power infrastructure to provide a new, high-tech future for this industrial site and will continue to retrain and employ workers that were displaced by New York's transition away from fossil fuels."[18]

It turned out, however, that what all that corporate gobbledygook actually meant was that the center's giant demand for electricity was not actually going to be serviced by new solar panels or other newly generated electrical generation. Most of it, by far, would be drawn from hydropower generated at Niagara Falls, power specially allotted to the corporation by New York State.[19] The cryptocurrency operation's hunger for new power almost matched the coal plant's old capacity to produce it.

The approval process by the Town of Somerset was heated, and there was plenty of local opposition. At the public hearing on the project, neighbors warned about noise (a notorious byproduct of bitcoin mining facilities), about light pollution, and about the further industrialization of a rural community.

But the people who ran the town, the ones who had taken on the task of worrying about things like lost tax revenue and lost jobs, they knew exactly the bind that the community was in. They saw the new crypto data center as the only way out. The chair of the Town Planning Board, Norm Jansen, said at the local hearing, "We just try to make sure that everything is good, not only for the taxes. I've talked to a lot of residents. One person here said they were for it. I've talked to more who say, 'We got to do this, we've got to get tax money coming in!' Now, is it the best thing? I don't know, but it's going to be income for the town that we desperately, desperately need."[20]

The sad fact is that once the environmentalists downstate got the notch in their belt for closing a coal plant they moved on to the next shiny object and never looked back. They left desperate communities to fend for themselves.

As a practical matter, the end product of all that much-touted Sierra Club organizing and rallying and activism to shut down New York's last coal-powered electricity plant was this: a plant operating about two days a month and producing virtually no carbon emissions was replaced with a cryptocurrency operation that will eventually divert an amount of hydropower from Niagara Falls equal to what could have otherwise fueled more than three hundred thousand homes with sustainable energy. It also helped fuel a rising backlash against the whole enterprise of a transition to renewable power. I assumed that all of that never appeared in any of the Club's news releases or funding appeals.

"They Are Coming for Our Gas Stoves"

In May 2023, legislation was tucked into New York's newly approved state budget that took aim at gas heating and cooking. The law would ban gas equipment in all new buildings less than seven stories tall by 2026. Taller buildings were given until 2029 to make the switch to electricity. The requirement was primarily aimed at homes and apartment buildings.[21]

Advocates, once again mostly New York City–based climate campaigners, argued that the move was an essential part of reducing the greenhouse gasses causing global warming. In 2022 a team of Stanford scientists published a study looking at how much methane leaked out of the stoves when they were not in use and how much carbon dioxide they produced when they were being used to cook.[22] Their figures were later extrapolated to suggest that gas stoves across the country dumped as much climate-changing emissions into the atmosphere as half a million automobiles.[23] At the same time the US Consumer Products Safety Commission was also issuing warnings about the way in which gas stoves in the home were contributing to child asthma and other health problems.[24]

"Just like we had to, a long time ago, transition from coal as your energy source, we do have to transition. There are clean energy alternatives," said New York's Democratic governor, Kathy Hochul, in announcing her approval of the new law. In the eyes of the ban's backers, gas stoves needed to go the way of the kitchen wall phone, a relic of a bygone era.

Alex Beauchamp, the northeast region director for the environmental group Food & Water Watch, called the move a historic step and declared, "New Yorkers are resisting fossil fuels everywhere they pop up. Now buildings can be a part of that solution. We won't stop fighting until we end our devastating addiction to fossil fuels."[25]

The New York he was talking about seemed to end somewhere just north of Manhattan. Reaction to the ban in Western New York was not so cheerful.

The backlash was led by Republican politicians who saw a winning issue, especially just months after the region had been buried under a winter blizzard that had left thousands of people without heat and power. Lockport's state senator, Robert Ortt, who is also the Senate's Republican minority leader, led the charge. "Out-of-touch politicians and bureaucrats in Albany are moving forward with a ban on gas cooking stoves," he declared. "This recipe for disaster is just the latest ingredient of Albany's unaffordable, unforgiving, and unsustainable climate agenda."[26] Reminding people of the recent blizzard, in which hundreds of families relied on their gas stoves for heat after power outages, the senator added, "These reliable, affordable stoves are vital to hundreds of thousands of Western New Yorkers—yet the political ruling class in Albany would rather blow hot air than look for realistic energy solutions."

Governor Hochul tried to explain that nothing in the new law did anything to take away people's existing gas stoves, or their ability to replace them with new gas stoves when the time came (if they lived in homes that still had a gas hookup). "Everybody who has a gas stove, enjoy it. Keep your gas stove. Nobody's touching your gas stoves!" she said in one news interview.[27] By then many people saw that this was likely just a first step and the backlash was in full gear.

Even Nate McMurray, a solidly progressive Democrat who has twice been the party's nominee for Congress, opposed the ban on gas hookups in new buildings. "It's not propaganda. People need gas stoves," he wrote on Twitter. "The storm kind of showed us that."[28]

The lofty arguments about climate change from people like Beauchamp fell on deaf ears in small cities and towns where gas furnaces are in every basement and gas stoves were seen as a safety backstop in winter if the power went out (gas furnaces require electricity to move the hot air from the basement through the house). Our local state assemblyman, Michael Norris, also a Republican, said that he had received more emails on the ban on gas stoves than on any other issue in the previous year. I heard the same from people I spoke with. One friend told me that her family was speeding up construction of a new home so they could squeeze in under the deadline for no new gas hookups.

The specifics of what was to be banned and when were no longer important. The mistrust and resentment by Western New Yorkers were in full swing against climate rules cooked up by activists on the other side of the state.

The Perils of a Backlash

No generation of humanity has faced a challenge quite like the crisis of global climate change. Runaway alterations of the Earth's climate not only amplify all of the crises we currently face—war, disease, poverty, hunger—but add new ones as well, like extreme weather and killer heatwaves. But unlike the crises we are used to, with climate change, humanity is less and less in control of the outcome. It is a crisis in which Nature bats last, and as we have already begun to see, a warming planet can be deeply unforgiving to the humans who live on it.

To keep the planet habitable for future generations we have to alter the way that eight billion people go about living key aspects of our lives. This especially includes Americans, who continue to be among the largest per-person contributors of climate emissions in the world. But people aren't by nature too thrilled about changing the way they live, including what the land around them looks like, what jobs get eliminated, and what stoves they can use. The effort to alter the habits of more than 330 million Americans in a more environmentally sustainable direction is made all the harder in the face of a deep backlash, a good deal of it needlessly provoked by climate activists themselves.

When climate activists don't listen to how changes impact communities and treat these changes as political bragging rights, resentment is inevitable. Eventually that backlash gains power. It begins to move beyond practical arguments and adopts climate change denial as a core tenant along with bogus tales of exploding batteries that can kill whole herds of cattle. It also helps fuel the election of public officials who feed into all that because it advances their careers.

Advocates for climate action cannot afford to ignore that backlash or to misinterpret it. They cannot just decide what they think is right and tell anyone who disagrees to "just suck it up" in the name of saving the planet.

What lessons can be learned from the rebellion against renewable energy in Western New York? One is that the people raising concerns about climate policies and projects at the local level are not all the antiprogress zealots or the oil company pawns that many climate activists would make them out to be. There are certainly people who "just don't want to look at a field of solar panels" and there are others who eagerly embrace tall tales. But there are many who are just like Margaret Darroch, the owner of Stone Hollow Farm.

For her, hesitancy about giant solar projects is an act of environmentalism. She, like many small farmers here, sees herself as a protector of the land. You can hear that reverence for Nature in her voice. Her concerns about paving over two thousand acres of farmland with glass and steel are legitimate concerns. I heard a nationally regarded solar planner recently who blithely explained that to meet the nation's goals for solar production we will need to spread panels across an area of land equal to the entire surface of Massachusetts and Connecticut combined. That means cutting down forests. It means taking away large amounts of land that we use to grow our food. It means a giant alteration of the landscape.

We cannot just dismiss the concerns about this as the folly of people who aren't serious. We have to find the ways to take action on climate and protect Nature at the same time. Some of the wisdom about how to do that will be found in places just like this one, where projects and policies are not just theoretical but things that have very practical impacts on people.

Another lesson is about the two chief tools of climate policy—carrots and sticks. When it comes to influencing the actions of families and communities, carrots offer great promise. Sticks, on the other hand, can create far more problems than they solve.

My daughter Elizabeth and her husband Michael are both happy about the fact that the solar panels they installed on their Lockport rooftop make their home more environmentally sustainable. But that isn't why they did it. They did it for the money. They took advantage of the generous state and federal tax incentives that paid for half the cost of their system and that helped them reduce their monthly electricity bill by more than 75 percent. Their story is emblematic of a much larger principle: if you want people to support and invest in what needs to be done, make them winners.

If we want communities to support renewable energy projects, give them free electricity in exchange, or at least fair tax revenue instead of a pittance equal to the cost of their annual fireworks show. We also need to listen to communities when they tell us that filling in thousands of acres of farmland with solar panels does not make common sense.

If we really want people to move on from gas stoves, focus less on banning them and more on making the alternatives a really sweet deal. When a state government hundreds of miles away starts dictating to people what kind of appliances they can have in their kitchens or forces a community to erect an army of giant wind turbines it does not want, what gets bred is backlash. When that government makes the transition to clean energy

A Rebellion against Renewable Power | 99

genuinely affordable for people, and a legitimate benefit to communities, it builds support.

It is also true that many people will never be especially moved by big stories about planetary peril but can be moved by the more direct, collateral benefits that those same climate policies can produce. I wrote and edited a good portion of this chapter in my favorite Lockport café, Steamworks, which sits next to the Lockport locks. One of the people that I often run into there in the afternoons is a fellow named Gene. He is in his eighties with a great shock of white hair. He is also a deeply devout conservative Christian, and while I write at one table he is often sitting at another reading scripture. (Gene is one of the people I interview in chapter 6.)

"So, you believe in climate change then?" he asked me one day as I looked up from my editing. I explained that I did. He handed me a book and asked me to read it and tell him what I thought. It was a paperback about the "climate change hoax," written by a collection of scientists who all turned out to get their funding directly or indirectly from oil companies. He complained that we were spending and wasting billions of dollars to fight a problem that didn't really exist.

I tried out a different approach. Couldn't we find common ground, perhaps, on doing things that are important to fighting climate change but also really smart things to do for other reasons even if climate change really was a great hoax? "How about making cars cleaner and making them use less gasoline? Would that make sense?" I asked him.

"Well, cleaner cars would be better for the air I suppose and better for the children to breathe."

There it was, the same lesson we learned at the Democracy Center when we looked at the strategies of effective climate action campaigns around the world. Sometimes the selling point for action on climate change should not even be climate change. In California when climate campaigners beat back a ballot effort to repeal the state's ambitious climate law they spoke about the impacts of dirty energy plants on child asthma and the urgency of shutting them down.[29]

All this went back once more to the story about the three blind men and the elephant, each with his own perspective and none of them wholly right or wholly wrong. In the years that I have been here in Lockport, I have yet to meet a climate campaigner from New York City who came here just to listen and to hear what truth and perspective might be found on this side of the elephant.

Chapter Five

A Castle of Old School Corruption

In the early 1970s, New York City was in infamously chronic financial trouble. This was the same era that produced one of the city's most memorable news headlines (in *The Daily News*): FORD TO CITY: DROP DEAD, after President Gerald Ford vowed to veto any New York City bailout approved by a Democratic Congress.[1]

It was the city's chronic financial troubles that led New York state lawmakers, in 1970, to approve a novel approach to helping the city generate a new source of revenue, one that did not rely on hitting up taxpayers for more money. They passed legislation to put New York City into the gambling business by allowing it to set up a network of neighborhood "betting parlors." In these new Off-Track Betting (OTB) offices people could come and place wagers on horseraces without ever having to wander far from home. Queens alone had ten of them.

Supporters boasted that the new publicly owned gambling system would serve two goals at once. It would generate much-needed public revenue (the city took a healthy cut of the action) and squeeze out the illegal betting operations of bookmakers (that seemed less certain).[2] What the OTB betting parlors did prove to be was wildly popular with gamblers. It didn't take long for other cities in New York state to want in on publicly owned gambling as well.

In 1973 it was Western New York's turn to get on the wagering bandwagon. The cities of Buffalo and Rochester joined together with fifteen Western New York counties, large and small, to form a new state-sanctioned entity called the Western Regional Off-Track Betting Corporation

(WROTB). It was founded as a "public benefit corporation." Over time it also grew into something else as well: a carefully honed empire of perks and payouts for a small cabal of political operatives who managed to seize control of it.

The story of the WROTB is about corruption of the old-school kind. It is a master class in how a small group of political cohorts used taxpayer money to build a castle of corruption that has withstood all questioning and all demands for accountability. It is also a story about the dance of power in a place of small towns and fraying democracy.

That story, though, begins long before, with one man and his dream.

A Racetrack in the Middle of Nowhere

In 1939, a colorful Western New York sports promoter by the name of William "Lefty" Goldberg saw an opportunity. He saw that if a horseracing track could be built on dirt-cheap land halfway between the state's second- and third-largest cities, Buffalo and Rochester, money could be made by drawing eager gamblers from both places. It could turn Depression-era betting and sports enthusiasm into cash. The result was the Batavia Downs racetrack, which opened in the tiny town of Batavia, New York, in September 1940. It grabbed a huge opening-day crowd of more than twenty-five hundred people eager to watch races and place bets.

In the decades that followed horses continued to run most weekends along its long half-mile loop, interrupted only by the external forces of world war and winters. During these years ownership of the track passed from one pair of private hands to another. That changed when publicly owned gambling came to town.

In its first decades of operation, WROTB remained a modest enterprise of small neighborhood betting parlors populated mostly by retirees who would gather to pass the day together, betting on the ponies and having a good time. In 1998, the agency morphed into something else entirely when it purchased the Batavia Downs racetrack for $2.5 million. The OTB betting parlors were small storefronts. Owning and operating a serious horse track, that was different; that meant real money.

Three years later, the New York Legislature granted WROTB an even larger cash dispenser to its expanding gambling operations. It gave racetracks in the state, including Batavia Downs, permission to offer gamblers "video lottery terminals" inside the racetracks. These terminals were really just slot machines with a different name and a lot of bright flashing lights. In 2005, WROTB opened up a newly constructed, full-scale casino just adjacent to the track, filled with more than 850 of these brightly lit video versions of slot machines. That casino now accounts for 85 percent of the agency's profits.[3] By 2016, the casino and track in a small town of fifteen thousand people was drawing so many visitors from elsewhere that the agency added a $7.5 million, eighty-four-guest-room hotel adjacent to the complex.

Today, the public agency better known as Batavia Downs Gaming has grown into a sprawling operation spread across 140 miles—from the center of the state all the way west to Niagara Falls. It owns and operates the Batavia racetrack, its giant casino, and three dozen off-track "betting parlors" and "easy-bet" kiosks set up in local bars and restaurants.

Batavia Downs Gaming is also a money machine. Over the past five decades, it has taken in more than $6.4 billion in bets and wagers and has kept more than $1 billion of it.[4] It generates revenue of more than $50 million each year.[5] Its profits from gamblers' losses are locked in as an algorithm. Under state gaming rules the glitzy video slot machines are programmed so that the gamblers, on average, will leave behind $8 for every $100 they walked in with. This produces a lot of profit.

Public benefit corporations like these are common in New York state. They are formed to run everything from toll bridges to power-generating stations. In this case it operates a vast gambling kingdom owned ostensibly by the taxpayers. Citizens, however, pay so little attention to how it is run as to make its management nearly invisible. The result is a great deal of money moving around, a lot of secrecy, and some huge opportunities for clever people to divert big sums to their personal benefit.

A Board of Directors and Its Expensive Perks

The responsibility to oversee WROTB, to ensure that it is run honestly and well, lies in the hands of its seventeen-member board of directors. Each member is appointed by one of the Western New York local governments that own it. Service on the board is a light duty. As one member explained to me, the work of the board involves traveling to the Batavia racetrack for a two-day meeting once a month. If they choose to, board members can stay overnight at the casino hotel at agency expense and eat and drink in one of its four restaurants. Under New York law, compensation for board members like these is strictly capped at $4,000 per year plus travel expenses.[6]

But for the members of the Batavia Downs Gaming board, that's just the beginning of what they receive.

Diehard Buffalo Bills fans are legend for the harsh conditions they will endure to cheer on their beloved team in the Antarctica that is the Bills stadium in midwinter. For the Bills' January 2022 playoff blowout of the New England Patriots, a packed stadium sat through three hours of football at temperatures of four degrees with a wind chill well below zero. My son-in-law and daughter were among them. These are not fair-weather fans, nor are they particularly affluent either. The Bills are a working-class team. For the loyal, being tough enough to sit through pounding snow on game day is a part of the job.

The executives and board members of WROTB need not worry about such hardships. They are not sitting in the cold. For years, they have sat snug in a warm luxury box complete with a great view of the field, free food and alcohol, and a tab picked up by the taxpayers of Western New York.

In September 2021, the New York State comptroller, the state's official fiscal watchdog, completed a two-year audit of the agency's expenditures for "marketing and promotion." The financial formula for WROTB is pretty simple. First, it takes in the net profit that comes from gamblers who lose. Then it takes off the cost of doing business. What is left, by law, is supposed to be distributed back to the seventeen local governments that own the agency to help pay for local services.

According to the comptroller's audit, over a two-year period the people who run WROTB spent more than $5.8 million on marketing and promotion.[7] One of the largest expenses in that promotion budget, by far, was the $1.3 million agency officials spent to buy more than five thousand luxury seats for events like Buffalo Sabres hockey games and those high-end boxes to watch the Bills. The purpose, agency officials explained, is to offer the seats as prizes to its heaviest gamblers. The seats were an agency strategy to get the highest rollers to gamble more, and lose more, as a way to boost profits. It is unclear whether anyone in the agency ever gave thought to how this might manipulate people who already suffered from a gambling addiction.

As it turned out, however, a good portion of those luxury seats didn't go to gamblers at all. They were doled out to members of the board of directors, to senior executives, and to their family members and political friends. The comptroller reported that at least $120,000 worth of those tickets could not be accounted for. The agency couldn't say who received them, but it wasn't hard to figure out.

Michael Nolan served as WROTB's chief operating officer from 2016 to 2020. He is a former volunteer firefighter and served prior as the elected town supervisor of his small hometown of Elma, New York (population 11,317). Nolan would also become something else: a whistleblower. He told me, "I would have board members calling me to ask for eight tickets to take their grandkids and their kids. They kept the tickets in the marketing office. If a board member was asking for tickets they got 'em."[8]

I also spoke to one of the board members, Phil Barnes, a retired deputy sheriff who represented tiny Schuyler County (population just under 18,000). He told me, "Board members would just ask, 'Hey do you have any tickets for Sunday's Bills game and they would get tickets.'"[9]

One repeat recipient was Richard Bianchi, the board's chairman and a member for more than twenty years. According to the comptroller's audit, Mr. Bianchi seemed to have a particular love of hockey and of taxpayer-funded alcohol.[10] In November 2018, he asked the marketing office for six tickets to see the Buffalo Sabres, an outing that also ran up a $1,300 tab for food and drinks. The next month he asked for four Sabres luxury box tickets for a gathering that ran up an $1,800 tab for alcohol and food.

Another former board member, Richard Siebert, represented Genesee County on the board for more than thirty years. When news of the luxury box giveaways became public he offered a novel explanation in a local interview. He said that board members and executives were just there to keep things tidy for the gamblers who win seats. "The host has to make sure it's clean," he said. "They have to make sure the food is served . . . we have to have staff members at every single event to do the housekeeping."[11]

These luxury boxes for Bills games come complete with VIP parking passes, special entrances to the stadium, private bathrooms, heating, and attendants to serve the food and drinks. They cost between $9,000 and $20,000 per game to rent.[12] It seems unlikely that the stadium expects clients who pay such prices to also pick up any stray bottles, cans and food left from the week before. According to Nolan, Mr. Siebert was one of the board members who demanded tickets for his grandchildren and whole family.

These seats in the warm luxury boxes with free drinks were a perk that any regular Bills fans could only dream about. For some members of the agency board and senior staff it was just how they spent Sundays in the fall. But these high-priced seats were not even close to being the most valuable perk that members of the board lavished on themselves at the expense of Western New York taxpayers. Those were the free health insurance plans.

The Buffalo-based *Investigative Post* is a nonprofit, independent news organization staffed by some of the most respected journalists in the region. For years, the *Post* has been digging into the agency's affairs and most especially the special perks taken by its top leadership. In 2018, after a long series of Freedom of Information Law requests and old-fashioned digging, the *Post* reported that thirteen of those two-days-a-month board members, and three retired members, were receiving free health plans from WROTB.[13]

The insurance plans that board members were giving themselves were some of the most expensive health insurance policies you could buy. They included full coverage for the board members and also their families. The plans came with no deductibles and no co-payments, but did include free dental and vision care. The annual cost of these Cadillac policies can top $30,000 for a single board member. For members who managed to stay on the board for ten years, as many do, they are allowed to carry this coverage with them after they leave, for the rest of their lives for free. It is an extraordinary gift by board members to themselves, one that comes directly out of taxpayers' pockets.

Jim Heaney, the *Post*'s editor and executive director, reported that the total premium value of all this coverage was more than $229,000 per year. "The workload is modest, as is the pay. But, oh, the benefits," he wrote.[14] Michael Nolan explained to me that after adding in other costs associated with the plans, the actual expense to taxpayers is more than $500,000 per year.

There is good reason that appointments to the WROTB board are hotly sought-after positions and that members hold on to them for decades. Appointments to the board are controlled by each local government's political leaders and are treated as valuable commodities. It is no coincidence that a half dozen of the most recent members have come directly from holding Republican Party leadership positions in their home county, including five county chairmen. In Niagara County, the county's seat on the board was deemed so lucrative that it was converted into a family inheritance. The county's current board representative, Elliott Winter, is the son of his predecessor, Rick Winter.

Aside from the enormous cost to taxpayers (all money spent on perks like this comes right off the top of what would otherwise be distributed to the local governments), there is one other big problem with these board health plans. According to both the New York State Attorney General and the New York State Comptroller, they are illegal.

In 2008, another public OTB operation in Long Island specifically asked the New York attorney general for an opinion on whether the agency could offer health coverage to its board members. The reply in response was unequivocal: "The board has no authority to offer health insurance benefits for or, more generally, to establish the compensation for its own members."[15] In short, the rules of compensation are set by state law, not the whims of the board members who stand to benefit. But getting that law enforced is another matter.

Not so fortunate in matters of health coverage are the men and women who work full-time to keep WROTB's operations running. This includes everyone from the janitors who sweep up the floors of the Batavia casino to the attendants who staff the agency's far-flung betting parlors. Just before Christmas in 2021, I spoke with a half dozen of these workers, members of the employees union. They requested anonymity out of fear of reprisal against them by agency officials.

These women and men do not work just two days a month as the agency board does. The people I spoke with regularly work thirteen-hour shifts. They staff gambling operations open every day of the year except Christmas and Easter. It is not easy work either. One of the people I spoke with works at an OTB betting parlor in Buffalo that was robbed at gunpoint in 2021.[16] He complained that the agency was more than happy to spend a fortune on luxury box seats and expensive health plans for the people at the top but then suddenly claimed it couldn't find the money to provide security at OTB outposts that are sitting ducks with cash on hand.

Unlike the lucky board members, the workers at WROTB do not get coverage for their families. At best, they get a high-deductible plan that covers only themselves. Michael Nolan explained, "If they want a family plan it would cost them $1,800 per month." In its negotiations with the union, the board has actually been seeking reductions even in that coverage, saying the agency needs to cut costs.

Antonella Rotilio, the representative for the workers' United Public Service Union, told me. "They are trying to take away the benefits of employees that have been there for twenty plus years. Our members are really upset, because the board gets to keep their own health insurance."

As news of the board's expensive health plans began to make local headlines, members tried to dispense with the issue by voting to eliminate that health coverage for any newcomers to the board but retaining it for themselves.[17] Richard Siebert, the same board member who explained that he and others only attended Bills games to do clean-up, expressed surprise that the health plans had become an issue at all. He told a local newspaper that "no one raised an issue" with the plans until news of their existence became public.[18]

These expensive and illegal perks and benefits to the members of the board were neither accident nor coincidence. They are pieces of a carefully constructed, taxpayer-funded castle wall designed to ensure the loyalty of all those who operated within, to one person most of all.

King Henry

The man who sits at the center of the WROTB empire and manages its many levers of power is Henry F. Wojtaszek, the agency's president and chief executive officer. Mr. Wojtaszek, a lawyer, began his climb up Western New York's political ladder in his hometown of North Tonawanda, a small Buffalo suburb a thirty-minute drive from Lockport. Wojtaszek started as a personal injury attorney and Republican Party activist and then parlayed that into being elected as city attorney. While in that post he also began serving nine years as the chairman of the Niagara County Republican Party and became a key player in one of Western New York's most potent political machines, headed by a former state senator named George Maziarz.

In his two decades in office, Maziarz became widely known as Western New York's unrivaled Republican power broker. He represented a district that stretched from near Rochester all the way to Niagara County, and it was here where his influence on local elections and local politics was most heavily felt. Maziarz also began mentoring two young men also from North Tonawanda who were eager to climb the Republican ladder. This included Wojtaszek, the city attorney, and Robert Ortt, the city treasurer and future mayor.

In 2014 all that backroom power brokering ended up putting Maziarz in legal hot water. A state anticorruption commission charged the senator with, among other things, not disclosing nearly half a million dollars in campaign contributions and spending.[19] Maziarz dropped his reelection bid soon after.

Those charges later led to criminal grand jury indictments against both him and his two young proteges. In 2017 Maziarz and Wojtaszek ultimately pled guilty to lesser charges. Word that Wojtaszek had offered evidence against his one-time mentor to get a better deal cemented a bitter feud between the two that would come back later with a vengeance.

The charges against Ortt, who was elected in 2014 to succeed Maziarz, were dismissed. In 2020 Ortt became the New York Senate's Republican leader and one of the most powerful Republicans in the state. Wojtaszek, on the other hand, left behind his ambitions for elected office for himself and chose a different path to power, one that led right to the top of a public gambling agency.

Henry Wojtaszek is a man surrounded by political connections. His wife, Caroline Wojtaszek, served four years as Niagara County's elected district attorney and in 2020 was elected to serve as county judge. His brother and sister are also New York judges.

His route to running WROTB began in 2010 when he joined the agency as its general counsel. In 2016 he became the agency's president and CEO. Wojtaszek is, by wide reputation, both charming and deeply clever. "He could sell the Brooklyn Bridge to somebody if he wanted," Phil Barnes, the agency board member told me. Michael Nolan, who served under Wojtaszek for nine years, told me, "Henry's paws are as deep as you can get into politics."

In WROTB Wojtaszek found the ideal platform from which to build and operate a political machine, one even more powerful than the machine built before by his old mentor. The resources it put at his disposal far outpaced anything a mere state senator could offer.

One of those resources was highly paid employment and contract work for his friends and political allies, which Wojtaszek turned into political grease. Emblematic of those sweetheart deals is one that Wojtaszek steered to a Republican political operative named Glenn Aronow.

In 2012 Aronow lost his job as a Republican staffer in the New York Senate amidst charges of sexual harassment of a female employee. The staffer accused Aronow (charges he denies) of "sexually oriented physical contact, gestures, threats and unwanted exposure to pornographic materials."[20] State taxpayers were then forced to pay out $90,000 for the sexual harassment claim against him. Afterward, however, Aronow found a well-paid safety net waiting for him in Batavia doing public relations work under Wojtaszek.[21] "We hired him on a contract basis to do some things and paid him $73,000," said Nolan.

Another GOP operative closely linked to Wojtaszek, Rick Winter, was awarded his own lucrative contract from the agency when he stepped down as Niagara County's representative on the agency's board, bequeathing the post and its Cadillac health coverage to his son, Elliott. The elder Winter's contract was worth more than $120,000, ostensibly to lobby state lawmakers on the agency's behalf.[22] Phil Barnes, the board member, who is himself a Republican, told me, "I quickly learned that the OTB is nothing more than political appointments." Lawyers, political operatives, and a host of other Wojtaszek friends were all given a piece of the agency's action. What they received was a lot more profitable and a lot more certain than any bet on the horses.

In October 2023 the *Investigative Post* reported that WROTB had paid out nearly $2.2 million to nineteen different law firms and lobbyists over the previous five years.[23] That mountain of spending built a castle wall of lawyers and lobbyists all paid for by taxpayers. The purpose of the wall was to keep at bay a rising tide of bad press, legal investigations, and calls for agency reform at the state level. As a political strategy this was pure genius.

The funds to pay for all this patronage and power came directly out of the pockets of the local governments and taxpayers who are legally entitled to the agency's profits. The Erie County Comptroller, Kevin Hardwick, told the *Post*, "There's a point at which it becomes ridiculous. It's good for the lawyers and it's good for the lobbyists. But it's not good for the citizens."

"It is actually a money maker for the Republican Party, and a patronage thing," Dennis Virtuoso, a twenty-year veteran of the Niagara County Legislature, told me.[24] Virtuoso is a Democrat who retired in 2020. He is also a longtime observer of the ways in which Wojtaszek uses WROTB to secure his power. "Henry can call a party committee member and say, 'Hey, you want to go to the Bills game. We've got a suite. You want to sit in a suite?'" Virtuoso said.

After I began to write about the WROTB story several people reached out to me requesting anonymity for fear of retribution. One told me that his sister, who works for a local politician, "is always being offered free seats for games by Wojtaszek." Another told me that after his business did some personal work for Wojtaszek he used gambling coupons for the Batavia casino to tip the workers. Virtuoso added that Wojtaszek also regularly directs agency business to local vendors who in turn support his chosen local candidates. "Take care of your friends, that's how you stay in power."

Wojtaszek's occupancy of the Batavia Downs throne also comes with its own deeply rewarding benefits that come out of taxpayer pockets. In 2011, when Wojtaszek joined Batavia Downs Gaming as its general counsel, he was earning a salary of $92,000 per year plus benefits. Eight years later, as president and CEO, his salary had more than doubled to $192,000 per year plus benefits, making him one of the six highest-paid public employees in Western New York. At the time, this was already twice what his old friend

Senator Ortt was making in Albany as a state lawmaker. This was nothing, however, compared to what Wojtaszek would engineer for himself later.

On top of his salary and perks (like free Bills tickets), Wojtaszek also found other, smaller ways to squeeze agency revenues into his own pockets. The 2021 state comptroller audit found that Wojtaszek had used an agency car for years without keeping track of his personal use.[25] That cost taxpayers another $3,400 on top of his already generous salary (an amount that he later had to repay). Wojtaszek faced similar findings about his improper use of an agency phone. The comptroller, Thomas DiNapoli, said. "Revenues from the OTB are supposed to go to participating municipalities, not to give board members and employees generous perks and other benefits."[26]

The legal responsibility of the board of directors to oversee Wojtaszek, and to ensure that agency revenue went to local governments, was far outweighed by free Bills tickets and luxury health plans. Wojtaszek made himself a fierce warrior to defend those perks and privileges for the board. That earned him a reliable blind eye as he methodically converted WROTB into the operational center of a political machine financed by the taxpayers' dime.

Banging on the Castle Walls

In the years since Henry Wojtaszek took over the reins of WROTB there has been a steady drumbeat of questions about the ways in which he operates the publicly owned agency and increasing demands for answers and accountability. Those demands and questions have come from many different places.

One of those was from Wojtaszek's former political mentor, former Senator Maziarz. Years after they were indicted together it seemed clear that Maziarz was still itching for revenge against the protégé who had turned against him.

In February 2019, Maziarz unleashed a set of corruption charges in a raucous televised news conference held at Lockport City Hall.[27] The one that stuck hardest was about the agency's expensive and illegal health plans for the board of directors. Maziarz charged the board with giving themselves "obscene payments" for their high-end health-care plans at taxpayer expense.

Maziarz said at the news conference, "I know some will call me bitter, some will say I'm trying to settle a score, nothing could be further from the truth." Wojtaszek declared the charges to be completely false and said, "This is a rambling by a disgraced former politician who is obsessed with trying to settle political scores with his political enemies."

Both sides were speaking truth about one another. Wojtaszek was indeed running an operation full of people handing themselves expensive gifts at public expense. Maziarz had not just suddenly woken up from a nap and decided to become a champion of good governance. His revenge efforts continued, including a political attack on Wojtaszek's wife, Caroline, when she ran for county judge and after that a taxpayer lawsuit against WROTB.[28]

The effect was to suddenly shine a bright new public spotlight on the board's health insurance plans. Inside the agency people began to get nervous, including members of the board who began to worry that Wojtaszek had steered them to take tens of thousands of dollars' worth of benefits they might have to pay back.

"They knew they weren't supposed to have the insurance, though they may say different," Nolan said. "Henry would just tell them everything they wanted to hear and the board just kept everything in place so they could keep their insurance."

In 2018 the *Investigative Post* confronted Wojtaszek with the attorney general opinion calling the board health plans illegal. First he claimed that he was unaware of it, then he defended the health plans, "The benefits they receive are hard-earned and well-deserved."[29]

Phil Barnes, the Republican board member from Schuyler County (who did not take the agency health plan), told me later, "It happened to be a board meeting time and we watched Maziarz go after everything—and the insurance was a big factor. We didn't trust the opinions we'd been getting from Henry." With both Wojtaszek and Chairman Bianchi absent, other members of the board directed Barnes and Nolan to seek out a new legal opinion, one that came from beyond Wojtaszek's sphere of influence.

That opinion came from the Syracuse law firm of Barclay Damon, which specializes in state and federal rules, including fraud. The firm's analysis was clear and unequivocal, Nolan said. "The opinion spelled out very clearly that the board should not have health insurance and if they continued, could most likely be liable for payback."

The Monday morning after that new opinion was presented to the board, Chairman Bianchi called the entire executive staff into his office to issue new orders. Nolan recounted what the board chairman said. "We need to be a team. You keep this up and the Gaming Commission is going to be after us. People are going to come after us," he said, according to Nolan.

Bianchi and Wojtaszek immediately stripped Nolan of his duties as the agency's freedom of information officer (which cut off his ability to share information with outside groups) and as its procurement officer, "to keep me from seeing the contracts," he explained.

Afterward, Barnes, the retired deputy sheriff, began to question other things about Wojtaszek's and Bianchi's management activities, especially the contracts handed out to their political friends. "I couldn't understand why we were paying all these lobbyists," he said. "We were paying out horrendous amounts. Some of it was $200,000 per year, some of it was $50,000 per year." That's when the retired lawman decided to take matters into his own hands. "I'm the one who called the FBI, and I'm proud of it."

Days before Christmas 2019, Nolan was fired by Wojtaszek. That next summer he filed twin lawsuits in federal court in Buffalo. The first demanded that the board members who receive the free health plans pay back taxpayers for the cost. The second sought more than $4 million for Nolan in damages for being wrongfully terminated from his job.[30] The attorney representing WROTB called the cases "political gibberish." Nolan's attorney told the press, "We're trying to recoup money that's been stolen from the people."

When the staff and board of a public agency like this are so compromised by conflict of interest and misdealing, taxpayers might expect the local governments that own WROTB to step in with some oversight of their own. It is, after all, those local governments that appoint the board and pay the price when revenue from the agency is siphoned off to the people who run it. But here as well, Mr. Wojtaszek managed to construct powerful defenses, none more powerful than the ones he deployed here in Niagara County on his home turf.

In 2019 as more allegations and evidence surfaced about financial misdealing at the gambling agency, Republican county legislators circled the wagons around their former party chairman. A county resolution calling for the state to audit the agency was batted down along party lines. One Republican legislator, John Syracuse, called it a witch hunt. "I just want to encourage you to continue on with what you're doing," he told Wojtaszek.[31]

Even after the state comptroller's audit was complete, with its report of financial misdealing, Republican legislators quickly buried a resolution calling for replacement of Wojtaszek and the county's board representative. The Republican chairwoman, Rebecca Wydish, said, "As chair, I'm not going to allow my meeting to become an extension of a political campaign."[32]

In the absence of any serious efforts at accountability from local officials, it fell to a group of committed journalists to do the digging. None have been more persistent than the team at the *Investigative Post*.

The *Post* was founded in 2012 by Jim Heaney, a former *Buffalo News* reporter. He jokes that it was founded with his credit card and patience from his wife. The *Post* bills itself as the only news organization in Western New York dedicated exclusively to watchdog journalism. Its depth, accuracy, and tenacity are legendary among local reporters. The *Post* played a key role in exposing the Buffalo Billions corruption scandal in which hundreds of millions of dollars in state contracts were diverted to allies of then-governor Andrew Cuomo. It also exposed an epidemic of lead poisoning among children in poor families in Buffalo. Since 2019 the *Post* has been dogged in its digging into the story of corruption at WROTB. I asked Heaney why he and other *Post* staff have invested so much time and effort into the story. He told me, "The conduct and stonewalling of OTB officials was striking. We kept uncovering a seemingly bottomless pit of misconduct."

The *Post* used a stream of Freedom of Information Law requests and other reporting efforts to tell the story about big cash bonuses for agency executives, the board health plans, the luxury Bills seats, the FBI's investigation of the agency, and the efforts of the New York comptroller and others to hold agency leaders accountable. Heaney said, "To date, we've published 44 stories, many of which also aired on Channel 2 [the local Buffalo NBC affiliate station]."

The other journalists who were keeping a close eye on the story and keeping the public informed were the reporters and editors at Niagara County's twin daily newspapers, the *Lockport Union-Sun & Journal* and the *Niagara Gazette*. The papers are owned by the same national chain and often share overlapping reporting and editing duties. The reporters at the two papers wrote dozens of articles chronicling every major development: the audits, lawsuits, news conferences, denials, and all the rest.

"We started taking notice of the inner-workings of OTB in 2019 when former senator George Maziarz went public with accusations about misuse of public resources by OTB officials, specifically tickets purchased for promotional purposes that were being used by OTB executives, board directors, their relatives and friends," said Mark Scheer, a longtime reporter and editor at the *Gazette*. After WROTB denied those requests for agency documents, another reporter who covered the story, Phil Gambini, convinced the New York News Publishers Association to help the newspaper lawyer up and keep pressing.

As the work of all the journalists was ramping up, state officials began to dig into the details as well. The most important of these were the two audits of WROTB by the New York comptroller's office. One of those was the investigation into the agency's marketing and promotions spending, which included the luxury sports tickets. The other looked at Wojtaszek's personal use of agency resources for himself. The comptroller had capabilities of investigation that reporters did not. The state auditor needed no Freedom of Information Law request to ask for financial documents. The office's findings were damaging. "The Western Regional Off-Track Betting Corporation needs to clean up its operations," declared Controller Thomas DiNapoli after one of those audits in 2021.

In 2022, Democratic State Senator Tim Kennedy and Democratic Assemblywoman Monica Wallace, both from the Buffalo area, jumped in as well. The two introduced state legislation to reform WROTB, taking direct aim at the small county power arrangement that kept Wojtaszek in command. Every county that had a share of WROTB, no matter how small (in some cases less than twenty thousand people), had the same one vote on the board as Erie County, with nearly a million people.

As long as Wojtaszek had solid support from those very small and very Republican counties, he kept control. The bills in Albany aimed to shift the board's voting power away from the small counties and proportion it to each local government based on its population, which was already the formula for distributing the agency's profits.

"Taxpayers are tired of the dysfunction that continues to plague the Western Regional OTB," Kennedy said.[33] Wallace added, "This is a public benefit corporation and they have a responsibility to spend taxpayers' money wisely and I don't think they are doing that." The effect of the legislation was also clear to everyone, Wojtaszek especially. It would shift control dramatically from Republicans to Democrats.

Wojtaszek and his allies went to work to stop the legislation. They used thousands of dollars of taxpayer funds to hire high-priced and well-connected state lobbyists to work the halls in Albany. Despite all the bad press and political attention, and despite Democratic majorities in both houses, the Kennedy/Wallace legislation died unceremoniously in the New York Assembly in 2022. The session came to an end without even coming to a vote. While it would not be the last effort by the two state lawmakers to untangle Wojtaszek's elaborate web of power at WROTB, nonetheless, once again the castle walls held.

Connecting the Dots

The reporting work that was being done on the WROTB story by the *Investigative Post*, the *Union-Sun & Journal*, the *Niagara Gazette*, the *Buffalo*

News, and others was solid. Every few weeks, it seemed, some new piece of the puzzle was discovered and carefully reported. But in this story I saw the same dynamic in play as with the Lockport schools' facial recognition system before. The work of the reporters was to cover the fresh details of the story as they emerged, and they were skillful at the job. The general public, on the other hand, paying half attention at best, gets lost in those details. It is important to also connect the dots, to piece all those details together into one coherent story people can follow and see as a whole. I set out to do that in two ways.

The first was aimed at a statewide and national audience. In 2019 I had become a contributing writer to the *New York Review* with a long article about events in Bolivia, "The Rise and Fall of Evo Morales." Afterward I published a series of articles that came out of my experience living and writing in Western New York, including a widely read piece titled, "A Liberal in Trump Land." In April 2022 I published a long article about the misdealing at WROTB, which the editors aptly titled "A Case Study in American Kleptocracy."

The article pieced together the whole story, from the rise of Henry Wojtaszek to the board's perks, to the unwillingness of local officials to do anything serious about it. I knew I was wading into treacherous waters, involving a man with a fondness for lawyers and an almost bottomless supply of taxpayer money to pay for them. My editor at the magazine, Matt Seaton, told me as I began work on the article, "Keep the receipts." This is editor jargon for "They may well come after us for this so document everything, twice." Putting the article through a careful accuracy filter was a part of the process from beginning to end—through two editors, a team of fact-checkers, and a review by the magazine's lawyers.

The article was also aimed at state officials to prod them to act. Reformers in Albany circulated it to all the members of the Senate and Assembly. In Western New York, the article made the rounds among all the reporters and editors covering the story and among interested local officials and members of the public who were paying attention. I would also learn not long afterward that it had also been closely read, and not liked, by Mr. Wojtaszek.

The second way I tried to connect the dots and help get the story out was quite local. As I was working on my *New York Review* article I approached Joyce Miles at the *Union-Sun & Journal* and proposed converting it into a companion series for the paper. She quickly agreed. At the local newspaper as well, the editing process was meticulous. Joyce took a close look at every sentence and every charge of misdealing with an eye toward careful accuracy. I was grateful for it. The result was a four-part, front-page series titled, "Shaking the Money Tree" set to begin running on the first day of June in 2022.

The afternoon before the *Union-Sun & Journal* series was set to begin, literally hours before the deadline to lock the story in, I received an email from Aaron M. Saykin, a partner in one of Western New York's most powerful law firms, Hodgson Russ. The subject line in the email read "Western Regional Off-Track Betting Articles." The attached two-page letter began: "I represent Western Regional Off-Track Betting Corp. ('WROTB') and write on its behalf. In particular, I was disappointed by your characterization of WROTB and its officers and directors in your April 6, 2022, article entitled 'A Study in American Kleptocracy,' published in The New York Review." The letter also made reference to a column I had published before that in the Lockport paper, "Third World Corruption in Western New York." The law firm accused me of "scurrilous accusations" and continued: "Your articles include several inaccurate and misleading statements, including outright falsehoods about WROTB's leaders, accusing them of 'graft' and 'corruption.' You are accusing them of crimes. *This is defamation.*"

I did not have to be an attorney to understand the thinly veiled threat of legal action. The law firm's letter laid out a set of complaints claiming that I had gotten my facts wrong, including on the legality of the board member health plans:

> You cite a non-binding opinion letter, sent to a different OTB, from the Office of the Attorney General. But, had you even asked us, we would have provided you with a contrary non-binding opinion from the Office of the State Comptroller, which previously concluded that "the directors of a regional off-track betting corporation may be included in a health insurance plan provided by such corporation for its officers and employees." At worst, this is a disputed issue. That is a far cry from your repeated suggestion of illegality.

The letter concluded with a demand that I "update the online versions of your articles to more accurately reflect the truth."

My first reaction as I sat out in my backyard reading the e-mail was panic. I imagined the worst. One of New York's most powerful political operatives, with an almost limitless budget for lawyers (paid for by taxpayers), was going to come after me and my family and every dime we had. I did not look forward to explaining this to Lynn. After calming down a bit I called Joyce Miles to let her know about the lawyer letter and see if the threat made her rethink publishing a series that had already reserved the paper's front page for the next four days. Joyce was calm and told me, "They are just trying to intimidate you." She said she planned to run the series as is without hesitation.

The next day I reached out to my editors at *New York Review* and sent them a copy of the letter from Hodgson Russ. I heard back shortly thereafter directly from the magazine's owner and publisher, Rea Hederman. He told me that he had consulted directly with the legal team that had reviewed my article and reassured me, "We lawyered this thing to death." The magazine's attorneys all agreed that the letter seemed much more like an attempt at intimidation than an actual legal threat. Hederman also told me that if Wojtaszek's lawyers did sue, it would be the magazine's responsibility, not mine, to wage the defense. With that I felt liberated to go back into battle.

My initial reply to Mr. Saykin was brief, asking for a copy of the opinion he was citing from the Office of the Comptroller, declaring the board health plans to be legal. Before publishing my *New York Review* article, I had specifically reached out to Wojtaszek and WROTB for comment, and no one there ever mentioned its existence.

What I got back was surprising. The entire legal basis for hundreds of thousands of dollars in health plans doled out by board members to themselves for years was a 1978, nonbinding opinion from the state comptroller. It was so old that it was written with an electric typewriter. When I wrote about the opinion later I noted that it had come out the same year as the movie *Grease*.

I forwarded the letter from Hodgson Russ along with the ancient legal opinion directly to the Comptroller's Office for comment. The press staff came back with a swift reply: "The State Comptroller has repeatedly and unambiguously informed the OTB that the old 1978 opinion was directly repudiated by this office years ago, as part of an audit report in 2007 and again by the Attorney General's Office in 2008 opinion. We urge the OTB to take appropriate action to recover improperly spent monies." The con game of the agency's legal basis for doling out health plans was stunning. With all this in hand, I replied to WROTB's lawyer with a second letter, this one copied to Wojtaszek, to every member of the WROTB board and every reporter who had gotten near the story. After quoting the rebuke from the state comptroller I wrote: "I can think of only two possibilities here.

One is that you and the leadership of WROTB remain somehow unaware that the agency has been 'repeatedly and unambiguously informed' by the Comptroller that the opinion you cite has no current legal relevance. The other is that the WROTB board continues to distribute millions of dollars' worth of expensive health plans to its members with the full knowledge that it is a violation of New York law to do so."

In reply to the charge that I was calling Wojtaszek and other agency officials "corrupt" I wrote: "The Merriam-Webster dictionary defines the word 'corruption' in this way: 'Dishonest or illegal behavior especially by powerful people. I and others—including investigative journalists, state auditors, and whistle blowers—have laid out a set of documented facts. If those facts describe a long pattern of dishonest actions on the part of agency leaders, that is a product of the facts, not because I have written about them." My letter concluded, "I will not be making any of the retractions you have asked for because what I have written and published is factually correct and well-documented."

A few days later a delighted Jim Heaney at the *Investigative Post* wrote about the exchange under the title, "OTB tries to stifle a critic."[34] He wrote, "Lawyers for the Western Regional OTB have sent a threatening letter to the author of critical pieces about the agency. The writer is having none of it." The article republished my reply to the lawyers in full.

While the castle walls were still holding, some of the people inside were clearly starting to get a lot more nervous—and much sloppier.

The Survivor

One notable feature of the legislative process in the state of New York is something nicknamed "The Big Ugly." This is the section of the annual state budget where governors and lawmakers shortcut the normal legislative process by inserting big changes in policy into the budget. The regular process of legislating involves a long trail of scrutiny and approvals through two houses and various committees.

Just adding legislation into the budget sidesteps a lot of that scrutiny and compromise. Inclusion in the Big Ugly is how New York has dealt with such major issues as legalizing marijuana and raising the minimum wage.

In the spring of 2023, the lawmakers seeking to reform the operations of WROTB decided that the Big Ugly might be just the ticket for getting around the agency's formidable lobbying efforts. Those efforts, which the agency funded at taxpayer expense, had managed to block reform through the normal process.

The budget language sponsored by Senator Kennedy and Assemblywoman Wallace, both Democrats, fired all current members of the WROTB board, effective immediately. It then redistributed the respective power of the seventeen local governments that own the agency, taking away some of the voting power of the tiny counties and giving it to Buffalo and Rochester and the two counties where they sit, Erie and Monroe. The oversight power at WROTB would now be divided the same way as its profits, by population. The language made its way into the budget and became law on May 2, 2023.[35]

There was no doubt what the political impact of the changes would be. It meant taking away power from the Republicans who dominated the small counties and giving it to Democrats. The change took direct aim at the political base on the board that kept Wojtaszek in control.

Republican leaders in Western New York went into overdrive to denounce the changes. Senator Ortt declared that any change in the agency's governance would have "dire consequences" for rural communities. Republican Congresswoman Claudia Tenney said that state lawmakers "should leave Western OTB alone and focus on the real problems facing New Yorkers."

The Wojtaszek machine was in full overdrive to defend its survival. Here in Niagara County, Wojtaszek's home turf, the Republican members of the county legislature went a step further than just news releases and public proclamations. They voted to spend thousands of dollars in local tax money to hire expensive lawyers and join a lawsuit against New York State, demanding that the reforms be rescinded.[36]

This might have been understandable if the new rules reduced the portion of the agency's profits that the county would receive, but nothing in the new law changed that. It might have been understandable if the new rules reduced the size of the county's vote on the board of directors. In fact, the changes actually increased the county's voting share on the agency board. That didn't matter. What mattered was that the Republican political machine faced losing a giant pig's trough of perks and privileges, one that fed a lot of their friends. The wagons had to be circled, from the county level all the way up to Congress.

I used my column in the newspaper to call out the county vote to use taxpayer funds to defend Wojtaszek's power, under the title, "Spending Our Money to Defend Corruption": "There are all kinds of worthwhile things that our Niagara County legislators could spend money on this summer if they thought there was some extra cash on hand. They could fund summer activities for our children and teenagers. They could fix some roads or sewer pipes that have been neglected. But instead, last week, 10 Republican members of the Legislature voted to spend our tax dollars on high-priced lawyers to defend the corruption at Western Regional OTB." There was a good deal of speculation, among those who followed the WROTB story, about Wojtaszek's fate at the agency. Some predicted that his days there were numbered. Jim Heaney wrote at the *Investigative Post*, "The power shift is expected to lead to the departure of Henry Wojtaszek, who has served as OTB's president and CEO since 2016." Senator Kennedy refused to publicly guess what would come of Wojtaszek's power but said that he expected the new board to "appoint people who will have reform-minded interests in cleaning up the corruption at OTB."[37]

Mark Twain once wrote to reporters in the US after he was the subject of a mistaken obituary, "The reports of my death are greatly exaggerated." So was the speculation that Henry Wojtaszek's Batavia kingdom was about to crash down around him.

On April 27, six days before the legislation coming from Albany was to take effect, the members of the WROTB board about to be ousted took an action that no board prior had ever taken. It signed multiyear contracts with Wojtaszek and seventeen of his handpicked executive staff.

"There were never any contracts at Western Regional Off-Track Betting," Michael Nolan, the former chief operating officer, told the *Investigative Post*. When asked by reporters for details on what the board had done with employee salaries, Wojtaszek replied simply, "We don't comment on personnel matters." Diving into the issue for the *Niagara Gazette*, Mark Scheer was finally able to force agency disclosure of the salary and contract information under the requirements of New York's Freedom of Information Law.[38]

There were good reasons that Wojtaszek wanted to keep the new contracts a secret. The newly locked-in salaries totaled more than $2 million per year, not including the generous package of benefits that went along with them. Nine of the contracts were for salaries in excess of $100,000 per year.[39] At the top of that generous pile of cash sat Henry Wojtaszek himself. The new contract that shielded him from being fired for three years and boosted his annual salary by more than $70,000, guaranteeing him a minimum (it could also be raised higher) of $276,000 per year plus benefits.

Wojtaszek's new guaranteed salary made him more highly paid than the governor of New York, more highly paid than the US vice president. These were not bad wages for running a public gambling operation in the far western corner of the state. The king made it clear that he would not be dispatched from his throne by anything as minor as state law. In fact, he just added more jewels to his ample crown.

The *Investigative Post* would later uncover yet one more amazing feature of Wojtaszek's new contract. It guaranteed him up to $574,000 in taxpayer-funded severance pay if he was ever fired for any reason. On top of that, if he ever decided to leave on his own to take a new job, he would still collect the difference between his OTB salary and whatever he makes elsewhere for up to three years.

Why was that important for Wojtaszek? One of his reported fallback options was to return to his hometown of tiny North Tonawanda and run for mayor, a public job paying $51,923 a year. Thanks to his contract, however, he would still collect a public salary more than five times that amount, setting himself up as well for one of the highest retirement pensions anywhere in the state. This would mean that the mayor of North Tonawanda (population 31,000) would earn a higher public salary than the mayor of New York City (population 8.8 million): not a bad deal at all.[40]

In September 2023, after all of this became public knowledge, I used my column in the two Niagara County dailies to write about it in the form of a letter of congratulations, "A Public Letter to Henry J. Wojtaszek":

Dear Mr. Wojtaszek,

In my 40 years of work around politicians and political operatives I have seen many who were skilled in the art of using public agencies for their personal benefit. But I have never seen any more talented at this than you.

Making Western Regional Off-Track Betting (WROTB) the base for your political operations was genius. Under the new contract you engineered last April you now get more than $272,000 per year plus benefits. You now make more money off WROTB in a year than 12 of the Western New York counties that actually own it. That is one sweet deal for managing a casino and a racetrack in a town of 16,000 people.

The way you got that giant contract is a true master class in political manipulation. It was like saying to the New York Legislature, "Hey, you really think you can take away power from me, Henry J. Wojtaszek? Hold my martini and watch this."

> The people of Western New York are not idiots. We know what greed and arrogance look like, especially when it is coming out of our pockets. Not even the most powerful political fortress can stand forever. Not even yours.

The castle fortress that is Western Regional Off-Track Betting had weathered investigations and calls for accountability from many places at once: from state audits and state legislation to public questioning and investigative reporting as well as action in the courts. But the castle walls still held strong. In the aftermath of the new state legislation, Henry Wojtaszek took to the airwaves in a series of local TV ads. "You have to love us!" he said cheerfully into the camera. The ads were also paid for with funds that would otherwise have been distributed to local governments to help pay for local services.

In the aftermath of a new board's arrival under the new state rules, Wojtaszek finally prepared to make his exit, but not without a pile of cash in his pockets. In June 2024 he announced that he was finally leaving his lucrative post in Batavia, but engineering a $299,000 severance payout for himself in the process. On his way out the door, he had one more act of brazen greed up his sleeve.

Wojtaszek had also cemented in the minds of others with political clout that heading the public gambling operation was a gig not to be missed. In September 2024, the WROTB board announced that it was hiring Buffalo Mayor Byron Brown, a Democrat, to replace Wojtaszek. Brown was handed a starting salary of $295,000, a big boost from his $175,000 annual salary as mayor, for a job with a fraction of the responsibility. One of Brown's more recent accomplishments was leaving Buffalo with a giant $50 million budget deficit.

One of Brown's first official acts in Batavia was to dole out a lucrative job to one of his City Hall cronies, Steven Casey, a man whose political consulting firm pleaded guilty three years earlier to a felony wire fraud charge. Elliott Winter, the Republican political operative appointed by Niagara County Republican legislators to represent the county on the WROTB board, declared, "We think he will be a valuable asset to our organization."

The corruption and abuse of the public's money at WROTB had officially become a bipartisan enterprise.

As I dug into the story of WROTB, it reminded me of something I had heard in a place far from here, from a grassroots anticorruption activist in Uganda. "Sometimes our public officials have confusion between what is their money and what is the people's money." That description could easily fit those in charge of WROTB as well.

I asked one of the reporters who has spent years covering the story, Mark Scheer, why it is so important. "To me, what's been happening at WROTB sums up almost perfectly why an active and responsible press is so important. You have what is supposed to be a public benefit corporation, emphasis on benefit, being run by representatives who used resources purchased with public money for their own benefit and for the benefit of friends and family members," he told me.

Corruption in our public institutions chips away at democracy itself. It taints every public enterprise with the scent of mistrust. According to a 2020 Pew Research poll, nearly three of four Americans say that elected officials do not face any serious consequences for corrupt misconduct. There is certainly no shortage of that here in Western New York, and the corruption at WROTB is one of its most shining examples.

I do think that there are now some serious cracks in the WROTB's well-constructed castle wall. Sometimes people become so confident in their untouchability that it is their arrogance, even more than their corruption, that becomes impossible to hide and to ignore. The political barricades in Batavia, New York are wobbling now. It may only be a matter of time until they come tumbling down on the people who built them.

Chapter Six

Conversations with My Neighbors

A community is like an orchestra filled with instruments of many different kinds and many different sounds. This is true of Lockport and the rural communities that surround it as well. One way to understand that community more deeply is to sit and listen attentively to those instruments, to those people, one by one. To add that kind of closer listening to this book I asked eight very different people to sit down with me for a talk. Each is someone whose path has crossed with mine in the seven years I have lived here—each in a different way.

These eight people include: a young Chevrolet salesman who voted for both Barack Obama and Donald Trump; one of the first African Americans ever elected to public office in Lockport; a third-generation CEO of a family-owned plastics factory; a special education teacher who became Lockport's mayor; a deeply conservative Christian who insists that climate change is a hoax; the veteran editor of the Lockport *Union-Sun & Journal*; a retired Vietnam veteran who serves on his small town board; and a one-time pink-haired punk rocker who became an organic farmer.

There is a good deal more to each one of these people than these quick snapshots, and that is the point. In a time of deep division we are tempted to reduce people we don't know into two-dimensional stereotypes. If we take time to listen to one another, however, we can still discover the greater depth that lies beneath.

My method in these conversations has been to ask a few basic questions of each and to then get out of their way and let them speak their minds freely. They spoke about how they found their purpose here, how they see their community, and how they see the country and its politics. There is genuine insight to be found in listening to what they have to say and some powerful larger lessons in the common threads between them, including about America in the divided time in which we live.

[Note: The interviews have been edited for length and clarity.]

The Swing Voter

Markus Campbell has been the best friend of our son-in-law, Michael Mulligan, since the two of them were teenagers. As best man at Michael and Elizabeth's wedding, he delivered one of the best openings to a wedding toast that I have heard: "First Mike went to the tallest person he knew, and he said no. Then he went to the smartest person he knew and got told no again. Then he went to the best-looking person he knew, and I couldn't turn him down three times."

Now in his late thirties, Markus has been married for thirteen years and is the father of two very sweet young girls. He works as the manager of a Lockport GM dealership, a place he has worked in one way or another since he was in high school. He now lives in Ransomville, a small hamlet of fourteen hundred residents near the lakeshore, mostly known for its racecar track. Markus is also a member of that tiny sliver of the American electorate, the swing voter. He voted for both Barack Obama and Donald Trump.

JIM: So, Markus, how did you meet your wife, Kiera?

MARKUS: On Myspace. Can you believe that? I reached out to her. She was from Barker, and I don't even know what I said. Uh, something impressive. We went to ice cream at Friendly's in Lockport. I picked her up. So I listened to rap music, had rims on my car, and pulled into her farm. She literally lived on a farm. And here comes her three male cousins and her brother. They're all on this little porch watching me pull in with my backward hat. I was eighteen or nineteen. And I picked her up and I said, "Do you want me to get out and talk to your cousin or your brother? "No, no, just leave!" she said. You know, the rest is history.

JIM: Tell me how you became a car salesman.

MARKUS: So I am thirty-seven and have been at my place of employment now for twenty-two years. I started because my father worked there. One summer he told me, "I got you a summer job. You're going to wash cars." So I started going up to Mike Smith [Chevrolet] two days a week, three days a week, and I washed cars outside with this pressure washer called the Tomahawk. And it was really fun, and from there it transformed into where I am today.

JIM: Did they let you sell cars at fifteen?

MARKUS: No, no, no, no, I wasn't even allowed in the showroom. It's funny now to look back on it, now that I am the showroom. So I did that for two summers, and then I stayed part time. And in 2008 I started selling cars. I sold cars for four years, and then I became a manager in 2012. That was a good year for me. I turned twenty-six and became a manager that year. Then I moved to Ransomville. So now that's what I do.

JIM: Okay, let's talk a little politics. You are this very rare breed of person in the United States called a swing voter because, as I understand it, you voted for both Barack Obama and Donald Trump in different elections.

MARKUS: So I know this might sound funny to you, but I think to me personally, they are very similar people. When Obama first ran for office we were coming out of the Bush era. So I was young; I think I was just starting to figure out life. And we were coming out of a war, and the world was very stale and then here comes this new person, Barack Obama. And he talks and he has charisma. I can't really think back then to what he had to say, but it spoke to me. It was what I was looking for, and it was a fresh change. So I voted for Barack Obama and he started to do a lot of good things. I worked for GM in 2009, and I sold cars and the government bailed out General Motors. That was obviously big; that's how I make money.

JIM: Do you think that saved your job?

MARKUS: Thinking back to it, it certainly did. At the time I didn't realize what was happening. Maybe I didn't understand how some huge company could be bankrupt but then they came out with the cash for clunkers and all of a sudden we were doing business. That was what I thought about it, and that's why I voted for him.

Then Trump came along and captivated another huge part of America. I certainly don't agree with what has happened or the representation that it has put on somebody that voted for him. I don't feel like I condone what he does. As a voter he just kind of spoke my language. Keep America strong.

So the Make America Great Again thing, that was big. I love America, man. I love my flag. I love my country. I love my military. I love watching a war movie, and like I cry. So I love being an American, and I felt like he was running against somebody that was in the party, that was just another kind of retread of a Bush or how we were going against Hillary Clinton. I just felt like politics needed a change. And I understand business a little bit more now. Maybe it was because he was a businessman.

JIM: And that appealed to you?

MARKUS: I felt maybe it was time for the country to be run like a business. Obviously there's some huge debt, the national deficit they talk about; that can't be good. I don't understand the money of politics and all that entails, but I felt like maybe this guy could come in and change it up a little bit. And boy, he changed it up a little bit. I never saw so many political slogans. People wearing political stuff.

JIM: So you feel like he energized and spoke to people?

MARKUS: Yeah, he did, and people grabbed it. It exploded. It became the main event. I saw it personally. I work with a group of people that are very like-minded, not like-minded like me, but they're together like-minded. Men, probably older fifties and younger sixties. They're all conservatives, mostly white, and they're hunters, gun owners, landowners—and Trump spoke to them and all of a sudden there was like a Trump sticker on a toolbox. I never saw a Bush, Obama, or Clinton sticker.

JIM: Did you support him again when he ran for reelection?

MARKUS: I did vote for him in 2020, yes, and then everything after that has derailed. It's embarrassing to me. It's an embarrassment that we're talking about him being in politics. There's got to be better people. I'm a registered Democrat. In the primaries [in 2020] I voted for Pete Buttigieg. Why is that? Because he's young. He could share a mind halfway between the younger generation and the older generation. But I understand that these guys, you know, politicians don't leave politics.

JIM: What are the two or three issues that are the most important to you, where you want to know where a candidate stands?

MARKUS: I always listen to what they have to say about health care. Because it costs me a lot of money for health care. We spend like $26,000 a year on health insurance. I understand that there's different levels to society and people need different treatment [different forms of subsidized care]. But I hate that because I want to try to be something in life that I have to pay full boat for everything. I go to work every day, and I work hard for what I get. Could you imagine if you didn't have health insurance and you broke your leg or what? You're in debt forever.

JIM: Do you think there are a bunch of people milking the system at your expense?

MARKUS: There's definitely people that milk the system on all levels and take advantage of it. And the systems should not be in place for you to be on the system for your whole life. I wish there was a way to help people get going in life. Um, but you know, the lower class sometimes stays lower class.

JIM: Why do you think that is?

Markus: I don't know. Maybe they don't know a different way. If you want to get out of it, you have to work extremely hard to get out of it. You have to get out of wherever you are from and change it. It's hard. It's like moving out of state. That would be an extremely hard thing to do. But people do. They move from where they're comfortable and they go somewhere that they don't know, and it's different and they gotta try really hard. Then there's people like, you know, the rich that just keep on getting richer sometimes.

Jim: Does that bother you at all?

Markus: To a point, yeah. But then as I learn about a business, it costs a lot of money to maintain the business. And maybe my view of who I think is rich isn't who is really rich. There's probably levels to richness.

Jim: What about these other hot-button issues that motivate people, guns, abortion, immigration? Do you have strong feelings about any of those?

Markus: I think guns are important. I'm more of, "Hey you can have your guns and you can do what you want, but why wouldn't you have to fill out a background check?" Like they're coming in to buy a car. That's all. It takes a process. You shouldn't be able to go in and buy an assault rifle and leave with it in an hour with a box of ammo and they didn't even scan your driver's license. That doesn't make sense.

Jim: What about abortion?

Markus: We lost our first pregnancy, so my wife had to have an abortion. I couldn't imagine being in a position in life that you couldn't have something like that. I don't know where I would not agree with abortion. If I found out I'm twenty-five weeks pregnant and I don't want this baby, right? That would bother me because I have kids and I view life as precious. I would guess I would go with terms; you know. There would probably have to be a certain threshold of, hey, that's a baby, right? Babies are born prematurely at twenty weeks and turn out to be fine. But these bans where it's like six weeks. Not that kind of stuff.

Jim: What about immigration?

Markus: I wish everybody would just come in the door and fill out the paperwork. I feel like if I was going somewhere I would have to go and fill out paperwork. As long as you're here to help America, there's jobs for everybody in this world. I don't know if there's a certain number of people that are allowed in or a certain number of people that aren't allowed. Maybe it would be something that I should know, get more educated on.

Jim: What do you think that people who aren't from here don't understand about Lockport and Western New York?

Markus: I just don't think they know us, and I don't know them. I've never been to New York City, and I've lived here all my life. I've really never been to a city. I think it's beautiful up here. I think our land is beautiful. I think the space is wonderful. We're Bills fans. That sums it up for me. It means I can accept heartbreak. I guess it would just be our way of life and our ability to do whatever we want. Walk around this town and everyone takes such fine care of their yards. It's something that represents us, the grass and the trees. I love my yard. I feel like it's just a little piece of heaven.

Jim: And it's yours.

Markus: And it's mine.

The Trailblazer

Flora Hawkins is in her late sixties and a native of Lockport. She became a mother young, with two daughters, and in her twenties she went to work at the Lockport GM plant where she worked for thirty-two years. She is also a trailblazer. In 2005 she was elected to the Lockport Common Council, becoming one of the first Black residents elected to public office in the city in anyone's memory. She has served the city since in a variety of roles, including as a longtime member of the City Police Board. She began our conversation sharing what it was like to grow up in the heart of the city's Black community in the 1960s and 1970s, in Lower Town, the section of Lockport down the hill from the city center.

FLORA: We were brought up on Market Street here in Lockport. Back then it was mostly a minority community. The other part of our community was Italians freshly here from Italy. We were very proud of where we lived. We were very proud of our upbringing. As my older brother said, we didn't see colorism like they're doing today. He said we loved each other like brothers and sisters.

We just loved it. We didn't even want to come uptown. We had stores, we had antique stores, we had barbershops. We had everything right there. [Governor Nelson] Rockefeller came. He flew a helicopter right there on Market Street and he gave all of us combs with his name on it. You know what I'm saying? Little plastic combs. We were so happy, we were kids. And then Liberace came to the antique store, and everybody says Liberace is here! And we had big families. We had eleven in our family. I mean, back in the day, everybody had big families, and we all lived in Lowertown.

JIM: Then what happened to the neighborhood?

FLORA: We stayed in that area until the seventies when Urban Renewal came through and they decided, of course, like they do in most cities, that they want to take the property where the canals and water is for tours and stuff. So they tore down all of our buildings that we had down in Lower Town and they uprooted that. They tore down our community. They gave everybody a certain amount of money to find another place to live. Then everybody had to go to different places. I remember people making comments about, "We don't like them. We don't want them where we live." Wow, I had never heard that before. I was hearing this type of stuff for the first time at my school. But we always made the best of wherever we went.

JIM: How did you end up working at the GM plant?

FLORA: I put my application in when they came up with the new civil rights law or something that they had to hire minorities. A guy came where we were living and had applications because they had to have affirmative action or whatever. They had to fulfill so many jobs with minorities. So all of us filled in applications and mostly all of us got a job.

JIM: Were those considered hot jobs to get?

FLORA: Well, yes, for us I would say that. You're not able to go to college because you don't have the finances. It was one of the better jobs. My dad always taught me to get a job that gave me benefits. He was always a stickler about getting something that you can retire on.

I started off on the assembly line. Then I worked my way up because I took every workshop you can think of. I worked my way to become a union representative. They gave me a job called joint training rep, which consists of helping give people different skills, education skills, like trying to help people if they want to do a skilled trade. That's why my education job was good because it was giving them different skills. I had classes for them to learn how to build houses, do electrical work, all kind of classes. If something happened [such as layoffs] they had something.

JIM: Tell me how you got into city politics.

FLORA: In the early 1980s I was appointed to the Citizen Advisory Committee here in the city of Lockport under Mayor [Raymond] Betsch. We were supposed to come up with different ideas to help with the progression of the city. He was a mayor, but he worked at General Motors too. I was one of those people that volunteered for workshops, volunteer for whatever, you know, to get myself off the line. So I think he paid attention to that.

JIM: How did you end up running for Common Council?

FLORA: This is a true story. I was asking God: What is it he wanted me to do in my life, and so I was praying on it. So and I said, if three people tell me the same thing, that's what I was going to do. So this guy comes in my office and he goes, "What is wrong with you? You know, you're not the same person and stuff." I said, "Well, I'm reflecting on my life and trying to figure out what I'm going to do with my life." And he said, "Well, you should run for office," and I was like, get out of here. Because, see, in the plant, all the jobs I had, I had to run for, so I learned a lot about running. Being a union representative you had to run for office and people had to vote for you.

So then another person [at the plant] came along and they said, "Flo why don't you just run for office." And I was like, for what office? I said because I don't know nothing that's going on in the City of Lockport because I'm so consumed with GM. I said, Okay, God, if somebody else says it to me. I'll do it. I'll do whatever it is you want me to do. I was just submitting myself to the Lord. I took my girls out for a fish fry and the waitress comes by and she says, "You should run for city council." I said, "What made you say that?" And she says, "Your presence." I said, "My presence?" And she spelled out my assignment. She told me that the third ward is open and I said, "Where's the third ward?" She said, "The west end." And I live on West Avenue. I got in the car going, Oh God.

Jim: Tell me about your first campaign.

Flora: And so these guys that ran against me—I ran against all guys throughout my whole thing—they were polished. They knew everything that was going on in the City of Lockport. I mean they were good. I was sitting there going like, wow. We had debates. Every time I turned around somebody wants us to have a debate. And I was being honest with the people. I told the people I didn't know anything that was going on in the city, Lockport politics. I came from General Motors. All I do know is if you elect me I will represent you, and I'll do the best I can. If you got any questions, I'll get back to you as soon as possible. That's all I can promise you.

Jim: Why do you think you won?

Flora: Because God told me to do it, and I had the confidence that he was going to see me through. When I campaigned, they all knew my oldest brother. My oldest brother died at the age of twenty-six. Everybody in the West End knew my oldest brother and they loved him. And I thought I was running because God wanted me to know about my brother. He died when I was like eleven or something. I would leave people's houses crying. They truly love my brother. And I got to know who he was through my campaigning. So I got confused for a little while. Am I running to find out about my brother? And then this one Italian lady told me, "You already won. Don't worry about it." She said, "God already spoke to me. You got this."

Jim: And what was it like serving? Were you the only Black member of the council?

Flora: First [recent] Black person ever elected to anything in the City of Lockport. I didn't think about it as a color. I thought about it like I did working at GM, a job to do. Get back with the people I know. It's important because it was important working at the plant, and people just care about you getting back to them and answering their questions and stuff like that. So I knew that part then.

Jim: When you were on the council, what were the things that were priorities for you?

Flora: Things that will draw people to our community. Because I was working at General Motors still, I used to use all my council money [the small salary received by council members] and I gave it for music festivals. Let's have some music concerts so people can come to our community, right? I had them out there at Outwater Park. It was called Unity Music Festival.

I would open up with, you know, gospel singers or something. And then as the day went on I had jazz and I had a DJ in between the acts. I had people in the community who knew how to sing or whatever. They had talent. I had a little open mic thing for them and they did their little thing, got a chance to do their thing on stage and stuff. So I did that for like three years.

JIM: A last question for you. A lot of people who will read this book have never lived in a small town, have never spent time in a place like Lockport, but see all this conservative politics coming from places like this. What can you say about that?

FLORA: I think Trump brought out a lot of stuff that I didn't, that I wasn't even aware of—his rhetoric and stuff like that. It probably was existing, but you didn't see it. The other part of what I always know is that when General Motors was working with ten thousand people and people could always get a job there and everybody was working, nobody was complaining. So when things go down and there are not that many opportunities to be at the top of your game then people start dividing. At one time it was so plentiful. Not only General Motors, but we had factories up and down where I live on West Avenue. If you lost one job you could always get another one. Then when the opportunities shrunk, then everybody started dividing. They start thinking somebody is taking something from them.

The Business Man

Bob Confer is the third generation of his family to run Confer Plastics, a company with just over 150 employees that makes products like swimming pool ladders, snow sleds, and plastic patio furniture. It is located in the small city of North Tonawanda, a half hour's drive from Lockport. The company proudly promotes itself as a family-run operation and a representation of the American Dream. Bob is also a leader in area Boy Scouts programs and a fellow columnist at the Lockport Union-Sun & Journal, *where his columns often chastise liberal state policies that he believes unfairly harm small and medium-size businesses like his. He also writes about his company's experience hiring and supporting immigrant workers.*

JIM: Tell me about Confer Plastics.

BOB: We celebrated our fiftieth year last year. We don't do any of the things that give plastics a bad name. We don't do any one-offs like utensils, bottles, anything like that. We want to make durable goods. Ninety-five percent of what we make puts people in the water or on the water. So we're dealing in what I consider to be good times. It's pool and spa products, kayaks, ice rinks, sleds. So it's a lot of outdoor leisure products.

Jim: What is it like running a business in this region?

Bob: There are economic disadvantages of operating in Western New York. I always say it takes 4 percent off of our revenues to cover the cost of doing business in New York [due to taxes and regulations]. We overcame that by making very large products that few in the United States can make and that no one overseas wants to ship. The things that make [Western New York] attractive for us are the cost of hydropower coming out of the Niagara Power Project and our location. We're within five hundred miles of 60 percent of the US population. And the fact that there is a long blue-collar history in Western New York that couldn't be found elsewhere in terms of skills, education, infrastructure, and resources.

Jim: How do you think this area has changed in the fifty years your family has been in this business, especially recently.

Bob: The demographics have been the major sea change that no one talks about. There's this misbelief that the labor shortages that everyone seems to be experiencing are based upon COVID and things like that, when in reality this situation has been brewing for quite some time. Whether it's a mass exodus of people going to greener pastures, whether it's for economic reasons—or, like Cuomo would say, it's the weather—I don't know what the pure reason is. But just like the rest of the United States, Americans are having fewer kids or no kids at all. I always look at school enrollment. Go back in time over the past twenty years. The decline in my school district has been at 27 percent. Niagara Falls and Lockport have both had a 24 percent decline. Those students ultimately become the workers. How do you strategize for the now and for the future?

We've changed the way that we make certain products, a fine example being kayaks. We used to make the kayak and do the handles, the seats, the bags and everything within them. Now we don't do that. We just make the kayak itself. We've told our customer in Michigan that we can mold the boat, we just can't put it together because demographics are against us. I don't want to have to fight with always having to access personnel that might not be there. So he accepts the fact that no one in the United States other than us could mold a boat for him, but anyone can put it together.

The other thing that we do—that we rely a lot on the federal government to support—is to ensure that we have a really good immigrant refugee population coming. Right now that is in Erie County [where the City of Buffalo sits], but I would hope sooner or later they start bringing them to Niagara County as well. One in five of my coworkers was not born in the United States. We have twelve different countries of birth working at the factory, living the American Dream.

Jim: Where do the immigrant workers in your company come from?

Bob: We have Myanmar, Sudan, Jamaica, South Korea, Vietnam, Thailand, Iran, Bosnia.

Jim: None from Latin America?

Bob: No, both because of the legal status and the way that the government handled settlement of earlier populations. Like the folks from Myanmar, they took them and said, 'We're going to put you in Buffalo, and we're going to put you in Fort Wayne, Indiana.' They had a plan going into it where now they really don't. So it's just making that mess of—'We're going to shuttle people to New York City and see what happens.' Before there was a plan saying, 'Here's the best opportunity for these folks, here's the communities they can serve, here's the communities that can serve them.' And we seem to have strayed away from that.

That is the major sea change that can turn back the demographics, opening up the gates to refugees and immigrants—just in an equitable and controlled fashion like we used to do.

JIM: This is a county that Donald Trump carried twice, and immigration is a big issue for him.

BOB: For a lot of people here, migration and the border is a very emotional issue involving a lot of fear and resentment.

JIM: Where do you think that comes from?

BOB: Some of it may be fear of other people that may not look like them, may not sound like them. I like to believe in the goodness of people. I just think that it is so many people are overanxious about how open the borders are right now and how calamitous it's been for the individuals coming across and for the nonprofits and the governments that have to serve them. Where maybe in the past it was more metered.

JIM: What you're saying is that what gets perceived elsewhere as an anti-immigrant culture may really be more of an antichaos culture.

BOB: Yes, because those are people's perceptions. What's happening at the moment is that we have a chaotic, uncontrolled situation. I always push the narrative about how important immigrants are to us. And those who are staunchly conservative always like that content when I put it out there. They value what we do for the American Dream, and they value the chase of the American Dream those individuals have. That's one thing that we talk about a lot at the plant is the American Dream.

JIM: One of the things that has always been so notable to me about you is that you're a businessman but you always seem to talk about not just maximizing profit but also what your business means to the community, what it means to the workers. Do you think that is a typical small business perspective, or do you think that's just you?

BOB: I may be slightly atypical to most business owners, but I think most small-business owners will have those same sorts of beliefs, just to a lesser degree. As with any organization, whether it's a business, the federal government, a church, whatever it might be, the larger they grow, the further away from the people they get. They lose sight of who they are and what they were formed for. That's why I like being the size that we're at now. I don't want to be anything above two hundred because then I don't know my people anymore. Now I know all their stories, their backgrounds, their names.

JIM: For people reading this book who might think of Western New York as some weird planet that they don't understand, and particularly the sort of populist conservative politics of the moment, where do you think it comes from?

BOB: When it comes to the populism movement and why Trump has been so popular, I see it in the guys and gals at the plant and in the neighborhood where I live. Because he's the first one in decades that's spoken to them.

    The Democrats had always claimed that they own the working class. But did they really? But now he's talking about jobs going overseas, production matters, farming matters, things like that: things that Democrats used to talk about, things that Republicans used to talk about. Someone's finally talking about Main Street. I have African American men that love Trump. I also have Latinos [workers who support Trump].

    If you get through all the bombast and you get down to the issues of putting food on the table, making sure that the factories are running, making sure the farms are working. That's what they see. So they look past the theater, even though the theater might be the defining thing for all of this.

JIM: What do you think that people in the big cities might not understand about areas like this one?

BOB: I think that many times people in larger metro environments tend to take for granted the things they eat, the energy that powers their living quarters and businesses, and the things that they buy. There's little thought put into where does all that come from. That's why I like plant tours like the one I did today. All those men and women had never been in a factory, that's a real eye opener for them. One thing that I try to do on our social media for the plant is to show that every dollar you're spending is impacting families here and making this happen, and we don't tell that story enough. If we did, I think people in areas where everything is brought to them would better understand where all that stuff brought to them comes from.

I've lived fifty years here in Niagara County. I'll never leave. People ask: Why don't you leave Western New York? The reasons are many. One is that my roots are so powerful here. I love this place so much. The other is that I could never leave my people because they helped build the organization that's a part of their lives. I can't take that away from them.

The Mayor

Michelle Roman, a junior high and high school special education teacher, served as Lockport's mayor from 2019 to 2024. She has been a teacher for twenty-seven years. First elected in a special election to fill a vacancy left by a predecessor who resigned, she was reelected handily to a full four-year term a year later. As mayor, Roman was a ubiquitous presence all over town. She was a particular presence in the tense aftermath of the killing of Troy Hodge by Lockport Police. She championed causes ranging from the return of city-run ambulance service to getting regular citizens appointed to city commissions. In November 2023 she was defeated for reelection to a second full term by Republican Jon Lombardi, in a campaign bankrolled by state Republicans who sent out a barrage of mailings claiming that, as a working teacher, she could not also serve effectively as mayor.

JIM: Tell me about your upbringing and how you came to be a teacher.

MICHELLE: I grew up in Lockport and I'm the youngest of nine. I had amazing teachers who made a difference, and I wanted to be someone who made a difference. [In school] they had a low group, a regents group, and a superior group, and I was in the superior group. But I was friends with a lot of kids in the low group, and they had the teachers who were burnt out, and I always had the teachers who were inspired and inspiring. I always felt those teachers should have been with the kids who really needed the motivation. So I wanted, when I became a teacher, to help those kids who were struggling so that they knew that there was somebody behind them.

JIM: How did you decided to run for public office?

MICHELLE: After the 2016 election my [adult] sons said that I needed to run for something. They said that my volunteering, as a VFW literacy volunteer and different things that I volunteered for, were all good, but I need to make a systemic change. So they convinced me to run for office. I attended a meeting that December for the local Working Families Party and they said, "What are you going to do to make a change?" And I stood up and said, "I'm going to run for something." That was when I said it out loud in front of a group of people.

Then I found out about this women's elect program, and it was women inspiring women to run for office and training them on how to run for office. I thought, well, I'll start with the smallest thing that I can run for [city alderwoman] and I ran against a very popular incumbent who everybody loves. I lost by eighty-something votes, which is not terrible, but I lost it. Then the next year the mayor of the City of Lockport resigned, and the Democratic Party reached out to me and asked me if I would be interested in running. And I was like, are you sure? Because I lost my election. They liked my platform, and they liked my message; they also liked my genuineness, and they liked how I ran my campaign. So I talked to my family, and we all agreed that I would run for mayor in 2018, in the special election.

JIM: After you won that election how did you look at the job of mayor?

MICHELLE: Everybody wants their streets, trees, and parks, right? Those are the main things. And then the next thing is their water and sewer. So it's mostly about the infrastructure—to make it a place where they want to enjoy life without having to worry about something going wrong. Very few pay attention or care about the backroom deals. They literally just cared about, "Is the pothole in front of my house gone, and is this tree going to fall on my house, and can my kid walk down to the park and play safely?" So I knew if I could make sure that those things were starting to be addressed, it would help in every area.

And I knew that we couldn't afford to increase taxes, so we had to get grants. We had to work with community organizations. I got a lot of people to volunteer. We needed to welcome everyone. You can't be exclusionary and want to progress into the future.

Jim: So you're a Democrat in this moment in which the Republican Party has gone sort of bonkers. As a Democratic mayor, what were your interactions like with Republican voters and the Republican establishment?

Michelle: I could not win without Republican support. A number of Trump supporters had my sign in their yard alongside a Trump sign. And they told me that they felt that I was like Trump, that I was an outsider coming in to make change. At first I wasn't sure how I felt about it. And I don't want to offend anyone, so I stopped posting any of my personal political feelings [about Trump and national politics] on any of my social media. I pulled all that stuff. I said, instead of draining the swamp, I'm going to clean the canal.

But you have the Republican Party infrastructure sabotaging everything that you do, because it doesn't matter if it helps the community or not; it has to follow their party line. During the [2023] campaign, people literally went door-to-door and told people that I was going to bus in illegal aliens and house them at the defunct hospital. You say it enough to people and they eventually start believing it.

I was at Cousin's Cafe, and this gentleman sitting next to me was complaining that the mayor of Niagara Falls and the mayor of Lockport were busing in illegal aliens to boost up our population numbers to get more money. I looked at the gentleman and I said, "That's blatantly false." And he goes,

"How would you know?" And I said, "Because I'm the mayor of Lockport." He was shocked that I was sitting next to him at a little tiny cafe.

When I was going door to door the first time I was running for mayor, a person that I know—his grandson played Little League baseball with my son, and very Republican—said that he should throw me off his porch because I'm a Democrat. He said that I was a "communist socialist" who believed in universal health care and open borders, and I'm antiguns.

I told him, "You know, you already have universal health care." He goes, "What are you talking about?" And I said, "You and your wife are on Medicare. Your grandson is on child health, plus your daughter is on Medicaid. You're already on socialism." I said, "Then the people who don't have insurance wait until they're so sick they have to go to emergency room. Then the emergency rooms charge an exorbitant amount to cover the cost when they don't get paid. So we're all paying that cost." I said, "So what we have now is universal health care that's not efficient and more expensive." And he looked at me and he said, "I never thought of it that way."

JIM: What else did you learn about being mayor?

MICHELLE: I think people appreciate the fact that I am honest. My posts [on Facebook] are lengthy. A lot of people complain that they're too long, but then other people were like, I needed all that information to make a choice about what my opinion is. I opened up our meetings to the public. I wasn't perfect. There are hard decisions that had to be made, and you're not always going to make a decision that makes everybody happy. But if you share why you made that decision and the rationale and the actual data and information behind that decision, people are more likely to be understanding about it. They still might not agree, but they'll say, at least I know why she did that.

JIM: What did you learn from the tragedy of Troy Hodge and how you responded to it, and how people reacted to it, like so many deaths around the country involving police?

MICHELLE: The first response is always the tragedy part of it and making sure that the family knew that I was very sad and that I was supporting them. Because no matter what the circumstances were, they lost their son, their father, their husband, their cousin, their friend. And the police department had also gone through a tragedy because they had to witness this death and know that happened while they were in charge. I needed to make sure that there was an investigation that was legitimate, even though it couldn't be as transparent as I would like. It's an investigation, and there's litigation involved and I was as transparent as I could be about it.

There were things that I started to put in place prior to that and then followed through on, and it was a catalyst for real change. We were able to add specific targeted training for our police officers. And I appointed three African Americans to the police board. The police started a thing with the high schoolers.

When there was a protest, there was a lot of potential for it to go as bad as it did in other areas. I walked with the family every year on the anniversary. There was one where the police came up to me, and they said the crowd was asking them to kneel in memory of Troy. I was not going to ask them to do that. They came to me and said, "We want to kneel with the group," and so they knelt. It wasn't them acknowledging any wrongdoing on their part, it was just them acknowledging that they too are part of this community and they feel the loss of this life as well.

It [Hodge's killing] brought back all the ways that Lockport has always been a racist community, and you can't deny it.

JIM: In what way?

MICHELLE: Like in the schools. Like the way that the kids are treated differently than other kids. They [minority students of color] get harassed more. The sports—my husband did Little League coaching for years and years, and he would take the kids who the other coaches didn't want, and he won every year. We had kids who were doing phenomenally, and they weren't even making the team and there was no reason for it other than their color.

Jim: What do you think that people from outside Western New York might not understand about a place like Lockport?

Michelle: [In more urban communities] there's a diversity that's just embedded in them, which is not the same here. Even though when I went to school, I had Native American friends, I had Jewish friends, I had Hindu friends; but they were typically one-off, two-off. If you wanted to, you could stay in your own little group and never branch out to those other groups. You would never know that that girl over there just celebrated her bat mitzvah. You could be totally separate here.

We have this backbone of, "We are Lockport, we are western New York, we support each other and we don't need any outsiders." But then that also closes you off to a broader sense of the world.

The Believer

Gene Baes is a tall, fit man in his early eighties (which he credits to his regular tennis habit). The two of us could hardly be more different or see the world in a more different way. He spent twenty-six years as a New York parole officer, is a devout Christian, and deeply conservative in his politics. We know each other because we frequently spend our afternoons having coffee in the same Lockport café along the Erie Canal (Steamworks), and we both appreciate the value of reasonable and respectful conversation with people with whom we disagree. I do also greatly admire his fire-engine-red 2000 model Mustang convertible with a horn that whinnies like a horse.

Jim: Tell me about where and how you grew up.

Gene: On the north end of Lockport. I lived on Church Street, right around the corner from here.

Jim: And you went to Lockport High School?

Gene: Yeah, North Park first and then the high school. I was always quiet, timid, like people didn't know I was there because I never talked. I didn't have a lot of self-confidence. I don't think

I understood anything. I felt disappointed that the system let me go through twelve years of education, and I came out without knowing what I should do next. I felt totally unprepared.

JIM: What did you do when you graduated?

GENE: Menial jobs. Actually my first job might have been at Chip Cigars and I was like a cashier and I couldn't keep up. So they let me go. At sixteen I started working at the YMCA as a lifeguard and a swimming instructor. I was working like fifteen hours there, and I also was working fifteen hours at a drug store as a kind of stock boy. So I was in high school and I was working like thirty hours a week. It was probably a mistake because I had no time for social things or pretty much anything else. But I wanted money and I bought a car. At sixteen, I probably had the nicest car in high school of somebody who bought their own car. It was a 1954 Mercury convertible, red and white with a white top.

JIM: What did you do in your twenties?

GENE: I had taken some interviews for Harrison Radiator, but I didn't know anybody and I had no pull and that's how it worked. So I didn't get selected. It occurred to me to call them later and ask them if there was anything else I could get into. They said that there were skilled trade openings, and I became a sheet metal sample maker at eighteen. But, unfortunately, I was ambitious and I decided also to go to UB [University of Buffalo]. I didn't have any direction. I took some night classes in calculus and stuff like engineering and to my surprise I was doing pretty good.

I decided that I would quit the job, go to day school, and become an engineer. One of the courses I took was chemistry, and I could not pass that. That was my big downfall. So that was the end of engineering. So I figured, well, I'll be a math major. Then all of a sudden it was way over my head, I was just totally out of my league. So I tried business and I did very well. But it was so boring that I thought, I can't work in this. So then I decided, well, I'm just going to salvage a degree out of this four years in anything. I really enjoyed the philosophy courses so I got a BA in philosophy.

That was really destructive to me. I was kind of a believer when I started there. I was brought up in the Lutheran church, and one of the instructors that I had, he was debating a minister, and he just destroyed this minister and he made him look really stupid.

Jim: What effect did that have on you?

Gene: It had a big effect on me. I immediately became an agnostic, right there. That was it. After eighteen years of Christianity I became an immediate agnostic.

But I knew I had a responsibility to research it and to find out whether there was a God or not. So I made a pact with myself that I would study atheist stuff for a year and study the Bible for a year. And I thought to myself, well, if there really was a God the evidence would be overwhelming and it isn't. So I said, that's it, I'm an atheist. I was a card-carrying atheist. I wouldn't let people talk to me about religion after that. I felt sorry for Christians that they were deceived, that they were believing a lie.

But the problem is that atheism doesn't work. You can see it in most atheists, they're miserable, they're unhappy, their life doesn't work. It took me twenty-five years to realize that. I did everything that I could possibly do to make myself happy in those twenty-five years. I sought out pleasure. I sought out illicit sex. I dabbled a little bit in drugs, not much though, because I was into physical fitness and so I couldn't go that way. Like the philosophy part of it removes your ability to know truth. There's no absolute truth. Everything's relative and you're just lost. And that's where I was, totally lost. I went through about fifteen jobs after that.

Jim: How did you become a parole officer?

Gene: I was always after security, so I would take a lot of civil service exams. By accident, kind of, I had taken the exam for parole officer. Then the civil service job for parole officer came up. When I got there, it was like dying and going to heaven. It was like the first job I had loved. It gave you all the freedom in the world. You came and went when you wanted to. You controlled your caseload. You were kind of your own boss.

JIM: So what does a parole officer do?

GENE: People that are sentenced to felonies go to state prisons like Attica. They get released early, like if they do a two to five [year sentence], they make it out in two or three and the remainder of their sentence is under parole supervision. We would give them a list of rules, standard rules, and then the parole officer could review the guy's file and make up additional conditions that he thought were beneficial. Like the guy was an alcoholic, so no alcohol. Maybe the crime was committed at two in the morning, so they'd give you a 9:00 curfew. So I would add like another half a dozen or maybe even ten extra conditions.

JIM: Let's talk about your faith. What made you become a devout Christian?

GENE: Well, the twenty-five years that I lived as an atheist, I violated most of God's laws. Probably the adultery one was the biggest one that I violated. I saw nothing wrong with having sex with somebody else's wife. That doesn't work, and I was too naive to realize that until the consequences came down. So I went through two divorces. When you're an atheist the world revolves around you. You worship yourself if you don't have God to worship. It's a recipe for disaster.

A church had a bus ministry out in Tonawanda Creek. They'd come around and ask parents if they wanted to let their kids go on the bus every Sunday to church. My wife said yeah, sure. So they went to church Sunday morning, and we would go out and have breakfast and just enjoy the free time. So then they talked my wife into going. So now she's going to church and my kids are at church and I'm sitting at home by myself. I didn't want any part of the church, but I didn't want to be alone, I wanted to be with my family.

So I got up the nerve to go to church and almost immediately I noticed peace and joy just glowing off people's faces. I mean, I'd never seen that before. I never saw that in the church that I was brought up in. And I was I was immediately jealous. So I got up enough nerve to go to the pastor and I said I want what you people have but I can't just face believing in God, I've got to have some proof, some evidence. So he gave me this little book. It was called, *Is the Bible Really the Word of God?* It was everything that I needed in there to prove the existence of God. That black cloud of depression just lifted off me.

JIM: How old were you?

GENE: I was forty-six.

JIM: Given your background and given how important faith is to you, how do you look at the political situation that we're in right now?

GENE: Initially I would be for any candidate that respected Christianity and God and God's laws. I don't believe that abortion is correct or good. So I would use that criteria to decide who was the right politician to vote for. But that was phase one. I'm kind of in phase two now where I actually believe that all politicians are corrupt. Trump is corrupt, Biden is corrupt, they're all corrupt, and they're all playing the same game. I think the whole world is deceived. The big wealthy people that control everything are actually controlling them and us.

JIM: What made you change your point of view to believe that?

GENE: I watch a minister from Hawaii who does prophecy updates. The other strike against Trump is the fact that he initiated the whole COVID vaccine thing. You may not agree with this, but my information tells me that the COVID vaccines are not there to help you. They are deadly and they are there to kill you. Because the people in power who are manipulating Trump and Biden and all that, one of their agendas is to cut the population in half. They're doing it by releasing this virus.

Climate change to me is a total lie. Scientists that aren't paid to get results [that prove climate change] will back that up. And they're using that as an excuse to poison the air. It poisons the soil. So the plants and stuff that we eat are poison.

JIM: You're not just talking about pesticides. You're talking about something else.

GENE: Yeah, I'm talking about deliberate stuff that they're putting in the air from these jets. Look up there and look at the jet with the stream coming out. If you can prove that's false, then go for it. But everything that I've seen backs it up. This is what people don't know today. They're trying to kill us. They're trying to reduce the population. They're poisoning our water. They're putting stuff in the foods. They're genetically modifying foods.

JIM: So what sources of information do you rely on that you have confidence in?

GENE: That's a good question. I kind of look at everything. If it makes sense to me, then I follow it.

JIM: A last question. You've lived here your whole life. What do you think that people who aren't from here misunderstand about a place like Lockport?

GENE: I would guess just the fact that there's more closer family ties and you can develop more closer relationships with people because you're not overwhelmed by numbers so much. I would never live in a big city, but I suppose to some extent you could do it there too. It's just more comfortable. Yeah.

The Editor

Joyce Miles is the editor of the Lockport Union-Sun & Journal, *the city's two-hundred-year-old daily newspaper. She has lived in this part of Western New York her entire life and worked for the paper for her entire career, rising from an entry-level position soon after college. While hundreds of other small-town papers like it around the country have folded in recent years, leaving places like Lockport in the dark, Joyce has been a key figure in keeping local journalism alive. Working with an ever-changing team of young reporters, she manages coverage of local government, features on everything from new small businesses, to the achievements of local young people, and other human interest stories that connect the people who live here. Joyce is especially a master of the witty headline and on the occasions in which she pulls out her editorial pen, she speaks with a clarity that is Western New York at its best. She is also the editor who daringly gave me a column in the local paper.*

JIM: How did you become a journalist in the first place?

JOYCE: Honestly, I just kind of rolled into it. I was a student at Alfred University. I just plucked communication studies out of the pile [of majors]. I took a couple of news writing classes and thought, this is fun.

JIM: What did you like about it?

JOYCE: Learning and figuring out the right questions to tell people what's going on. That's just what I liked about it.

JIM: And what did you do after you graduated?

JOYCE: Well, I wandered around for a little while, and then there was an opening at the newspaper and the composing room. Not in the newsroom at the time. I took it, at the *Union-Sun & Journal*, just to get my foot in the door.

JIM: How old were you then?

JOYCE: Twenty-two, and I worked in composing for a few years and then I ended up going over to the newsroom as a graphics person. And within a couple of months I was writing.

JIM: What were the first stories you wrote about?

JOYCE: I think I got sent to some town board meetings. I ended up covering pretty much every beat in our area—pretty much everything at some point.

JIM: How long were you a reporter?

JOYCE: Probably for three years before I became an editor, and I went to Medina to the *Journal-Register* [a smaller sister newspaper, since closed] and was the editor there. Then I was jealous of the reporters because they got to go out every day. I decided to be a reporter again and I came back to Lockport, covering the city government, the school district and I think the county was in there too, and just whatever needed doing.

JIM: How has local journalism in this area changed over the time you've been involved in it?

JOYCE: Well, there are fewer of us telling stories, and there doesn't seem to be as much demand for community news. Over time, certain traditional offerings of the print newspaper—weddings and engagements and the happy, fluffy stuff, what we used to call refrigerator art—people took charge of that themselves. You can put your own news on your Facebook or any other social media platform. It doesn't matter that we buy ink by the barrel anymore, because everybody does in a way. So the challenge now is to figure out what sorts of news and information fewer customers want from us, need from us, and will pay to keep receiving from us.

JIM: What about people in their twenties and thirties and even forties and the newspaper? Do you see them walking away from the newspaper as a source of information? Is it generational or is it something else?

JOYCE: To an extent, it is generational. But this takes me back to the question of how we figure out what people want from us. It's the daily challenge. We just had this conversation in a staff meeting yesterday, and I freely admit, most days I'm not sure what our customers want from us anymore. They don't want [local government] meeting reports. We know generally they like people stories. You know, content that celebrates accomplishments and things that are unique about our friends and our neighbors. The political stuff is much more tricky.

JIM: How so?

Joyce: I'll take it back to 2008, in the election of Barack Obama. Prior to that election we had a number of calls to the newsroom from people who didn't identify themselves and wanted to know if we were endorsing in the presidential election and if we had decided. They would say weird things like, "Well, I'll stay tuned, because, you know, depending on who you choose I will decide whether I'm going to continue buying your newspaper or not."

Jim: Is your presumption that they would be mad if you endorsed one candidate or the other?

Joyce: Oh, I assumed they were going to be mad when we endorsed Barack Obama, which we did. We've gotten out of endorsements since, well, after 2016. There are a lot of examples. You know, somebody might come in and take exception to this columnist or that local columnist. As an editorial page editor I don't expect anyone to conform to my beliefs in order to get published. I like to be challenged. I would like to have the range. The buffet doesn't go over well with a lot of readers though. People want to read what they already believe to be true.

Jim: So what you're saying is that as the country has gotten more and more polarized and as national media has become more about feeding people partisan red meat, there are people who look at local newspapers with the same expectation of, "Which side are you on?"

Joyce: Yes, it's, "You're obviously on a side, everybody's on a side." There is no such thing as a buffet and it doesn't matter whether ninety things you do are not on a side. If you do publish somebody who's taken a side, then oh, the paper's obviously a left-wing rag.

Jim: What about the relationship between the paper and local politics? How important is it to you as the editor that the newspaper be on top of what's happening with local politics and local government?

Joyce: Well, I feel like that's a main responsibility. The service we provide or the thing that we try to do is give you the information to help you navigate your world. We talk about how meeting stories are so boring. As a reporter, you go to these public meetings and you simply listen, to understand. You know where something is brewing that you might be able to help people understand better if you start asking some questions. You understand the sides of an argument that's ongoing. But we're selective about what we choose to devote resources to because there are so many fewer of us now than there used to be.

Generally, I ask the reporters to identify things that people will care about because it has some impact on them. Who the new mayor appoints to the planning board or whatever, it's all inside baseball. But it's very clear most people don't like inside baseball. What's the effect on your pocketbook, on your quality of life, on your neighborhood? Those are the stories that we go after.

JIM: When you think about the last few years, what are the local stories in Lockport that people here saw themselves being affected by?

JOYCE: The obvious one is the reformation of the ambulance service [the privatized ambulance service was replaced with one operated by the city].

JIM: Why is that?

JOYCE: It isn't just a political thing. The private industry was falling apart. I mean that really, if you can call 911 and nobody's coming, what the hell are you going to do? That's a big deal.

JIM: And that's the kind of thing that readers would care about.

JOYCE: In two directions. It's both a personal safety issue and a money issue as a taxpayer.

JIM: Shifting gears a bit. There's a lot of discussion in the national media these days about the demise of local journalism. And here you are, still plugging away and having a local paper. How is it that this paper has stayed alive? Why do we still have a paper when so many other communities don't?

JOYCE: Well, the newspaper has an owner [the CNHI newspaper chain] that wants it to survive as long as it can provide the return on investment that is expected. And we sell ads.

JIM: Who buys ads?

JOYCE: It's more and more the case of small businesses, really, and maybe some regional entities. I think people who do business with the newspaper and buy the newspaper have a common understanding that if you want this to continue, you have to invest in it. Our strongest supporters, whether they are subscribers or advertisers, understand that they're not just buying ad space or buying a subscription, they're investing in this.

We are committed to neutrality, objectivity. There is no such thing as total objectivity, you know. I forget who said that, but it's true. Everybody has their filters. But we're certainly more committed to that goal than anyone else around us. But increasingly the tone is, "Oh, you know, you're that liberal rag."

JIM: Why is that?

JOYCE: I don't know, because they heard it on Fox, I guess. You know, it just becomes like if you say it often enough or you hear it often enough, it must be true. Because it doesn't sound like Fox. If it doesn't sound like Fox, it must be a liberal perspective.

The Veteran

Jon Hotaling is in his late seventies and a native of the small town of Somerset, north of Lockport along the shore of Lake Ontario, where he still lives today. He is a veteran of the Vietnam War and spent a good portion of his youth in the US Air Force serving as an aircraft mechanic in posts across Asia. His military service and his activities since in veterans organizations is a big part of his identity. His photo as a young serviceman is on a giant placard on a town light post as part of the Hometown Heroes project. In his civilian life he worked as a foreman for Cummins, a major national engines manufacturer, working his way up from the shop floor. He has also served in various local government posts in Barker, including a long stint on the Town Board. Jon is a staple at the Lockport Community Market selling items that range from handmade wooden tables to lamps made out of trumpets. The market is where I have known Jon, since not long after my arrival in Lockport.

JIM: Tell me a bit about your background.

JON: Basically. I was born and raised in Somerset. I graduated from Barker Central High School [Somerset and Barker are essentially one community]. I shortly thereafter enlisted in the Air Force, did eight years. Served overseas in Vietnam, Korea, the Philippines, and Japan. Short stints in each but more time in Korea than anywhere else. I've made a very comfortable living as a mechanic. I retired as a supervisor from a Cummins engine shop in Buffalo. I was a shop foreman up there for fifteen years, but I started on the floor and then worked my way up.

JIM: What was your childhood like?

JON: My father was killed in 1955. Truck accident. He was a trucker. I was eight years old and my mother basically brought us up. I had an older sister. She was old enough that we were too far apart and were never really close. I basically brought myself up because my mother worked a lot of hours and a lot of days. She was a laborer at Southland Frozen Foods.

When I grew up in the town of Somerset, the village of Barker was booming. There were businesses everywhere. There were lumber companies. There were hardware stores, grocery stores. There were clothing stores, a shoe store, appliance store, you name it . . . restaurants. It was all there. Three service stations, two car dealerships. Eventually it just drifted away.

JIM: Why?

JON: I think the advent of the modern automobile changed things a lot. The railroad and the buses quit coming and the like. Harrison radiator, you went to work for any of those companies, you were making maybe $1.50 an hour. I went to work for a brief six months at Harrison Rader in 1965, it was a $3-an-hour job. Then I joined the military and did eight years in the service.

JIM: What made you want to enlist?

JON: I wanted to volunteer and help my country. My grandfather and my great grandfather and my father all served in the United States military. So I was fourth generation. I had one Civil War, World War I, World War II, and me.

JIM: How did your service change you?

JON: It gave me a purpose and a lot of discipline that I didn't have before, that I never grew up with. I thoroughly enjoyed the military. I was an aircraft mechanic. I got honored as crew chief of the year for the 75th Fighter Wing. Then my second hitch was up. They were going to send me to Kansas, and I said, what the hell is in Kansas? So my plan was to come home. You could be home for up to ninety days, go right back in, lose nothing.

JIM: Why didn't you go back in?

JON: Okay, in that ninety days, I met, fell in love, and married my wife.

JIM: All in ninety days? Wow, that was quick!

JON: All in ninety days, yes. Our first date was November 22. We got married on Valentine's Day. We've been married forty-eight years.

JIM: How did you get involved in local government?

JON: I got approached in the mid-1980s to serve on a few ad hoc committees and it was very rewarding, very interesting. In the late 1980s, I got appointed to the zoning board of appeals. And then they needed a person on the planning board, so I went on the planning board, and I was on the planning board for twenty years, fifteen as chairman. When I retired, there was an opening on the town board, and I was called and asked if I would like to be on it. I am now on my third term as councilman on the town board.

JIM: Is that appointed or do you run for that?

JON: Elected

JIM: How do you campaign?

JON: I go door to door when I petition [for the required signatures to be on the ballot] and talk to everybody. Most of the people know who I am.

JIM: Let's talk a bit about the [Kintigh Generating Station] power plant. What was your reaction when the downstate environmentalists decided they were going to go after the plant?

JON: I was fully in favor of the plant. It was the cleanest coal-fired power plant in the United States. And Cuomo decided that we didn't need coal-fired plants anymore. I was not happy about it. They employed almost two hundred people down there. The majority of them lived in the town, union jobs.

JIM: What effect did it have when they closed the coal plant?

JON: Well, some guys got other jobs. Other guys moved out. On the town the effect was that we lost the pilot agreement [the payment agreement in lieu of taxes].

JIM: How much of the town's resources came from that pilot? Was it a lot of money?

JON: It was, maybe 20 percent [of the town's budget.]

JIM: What can you tell me about the Republican Party here in Niagara County?

Jon: In the 60s, in the 1970s, and maybe even into the 1980s, Niagara Falls was controlled by the Mafia and the Niagara County Republican Party. It was not above board. We'll just say it that way. Under previous [party leaders] like Senator Maziarz and that individual you wrote about that heads up the off-track betting over in Batavia [Henry Wojtaszek], who was at that time chairman of the Republican committee in Niagara County, the statement was made that the crooked Democrat Party in Albany is taking lessons from the Republicans in Niagara County. That's changed.

Jim: How is it different now?

Jon: It's changed a lot. The county legislators have all changed, there's some really good ones in there now. That's totally different than what it was, even, I'll say ten years ago. Way more honest.

Jim: What can you say about the rise of Trumpism in the county. He's very popular here. What is his appeal?

Jon: His making Make America Great Again slogan. What he did in 2016 when he started out it was really a big draw.

Jim: Why is that? What is it about that that's so appealing to people?

Jon: Thinking they were going to get more money in their pocket. I mean, that's the whole thing.

Jim: What do you think about the condition of the country today?

Jon: The condition of this country is, as far as I'm concerned, is going to hell in a handbasket.

Jim: What are some of the things that you see that make you feel that way.

Jon: The economy and immigration. Something's got to be done there. I don't deny those people what they want to do and why they want to come here. But something's got to be done. I mean, we had Ellis Island for years and all. I mean, we're all immigrants. We're all descendants of immigrants, you know, but come in legally. They just keep crashing through the border and there's no control. Yeah, like I said, I don't begrudge those people a thing. They want to come for a better life.

JIM: What do you love about where you live?

JON: The friendliness, the ruralness, the quietness. I used to know probably everybody in the town.

JIM: Can you tell me a bit about your work with veterans in your community?

JON: Our American Legion is very small. It's a small community, and we don't have a lot of money, but we do several projects. We do an empowerment program where if there's a veteran in need, we have a $500 fund where we can give them help. We do a fantastic Memorial Day service. We now do the Hometown Heroes [posters project]. We give out a very nice high school scholarship to a senior high school student every year. We're very community minded.

I'm very proud of my country. I always have been a proud American. Otherwise I wouldn't have joined the service to start with.

The Farmer

Kristi Winquist is the owner and operator, with her husband Jerry, of Local Roots Farm, a small organic operation in the tiny Niagara County hamlet of Burt (population 1,556). In her mid-thirties, she is the mother of a ten-year-old boy, and grew up in the nearby town of Newfane before moving to Lockport during high school. She describes herself as a one-time, pink-haired punk rocker who found her passion in working the soil. During summers the farm's well-known green mini-bus with Kristi and Jerry in it, is a weekly presence at Lockport's Community Market, selling the organic produce from the farm. Kristi spoke to me as she took a break from transplanting four hundred spinach seedlings.

Jim: Let's start off with a bit of your background. Where did you grow up? What were you like as a kid?

Kristi: ADHD (Attention deficit hyperactivity disorder), I hate to go there, but I struggled and still I would say I strive now with ADHD. But as a child I struggled with hyperactivity and being a little different. My childhood was 'keep the hyper kid busy.' So I played a lot of hockey. I was in music. I played soccer. I played high school lacrosse. I was also a rebellious kid. I was the first person in my graduating class to get a tattoo. I had my nose pierced when I was fourteen without any permission. I tended to go to the rhythm of my own beat. Little did I know that I was just in a small town, and there were a lot of other folks like me.

After high school I ended up going to college at N triple C [Niagara County Community College, since renamed SUNY Niagara] for a little bit. Went from there to Buff State. Didn't like it. Dropped out of Buff State within the first week of going there. My focus was on education because at the time I really thought I was going to be a teacher. Honestly, what did it for me was the parking situation. I guarantee if I had an easier way to park my car at Buff State, I probably would have stayed. As weird as that is. It's one of those weird ADHD things. I found a full-time job and jumped into professional life really young.

Jim: That's when you went to work at People Inc. [a local non-profit that supports people with disabilities and special needs]?

Kristi: [At first] I was working overnight shifts when most of the individuals and group homes were asleep. But over the years there I moved up to direct care and to primary instructor and this was what I was looking for. I was teaching. I was using music. I was helping individuals with difficulties with literacy. So I would help folks learn to read and learn to write a little bit. But when I had my son my focus shifted, and I realized that I wasn't giving my students and the individuals I cared for 100 percent of my devotion. So I stepped down and I found a replacement for myself, who I am so happy to say is still there and kicking butt.

JIM: So how did you decide to become a farmer?

KRISTI: I was honestly super inspired by Abby [Abby Kenzie, one of Kristi's closest friends]. We always had a small garden, but Abby had chickens. I was like, wow, I can't even say I'm a farmer if I don't have chickens. I ended up getting chickens because Abby inspired me, and slowly every day I would get more drawn to being home with the chickens, being home with my son, being in the garden, making my own food, growing my own food for the family. Ever since I was a little kid I remember my parents asking me, "What do you want to be when you grow up?" I would say ludicrous things like, "I want to be a mermaid. I want to be a rock star. And I guess maybe farmer would be cool because you're your own boss."

When I married Jerry, he really opened my eyes to the possibility of possibilities, that you could do whatever you want. Like money, yeah, it's a hurdle, but if you work hard enough and stick your nose to the grindstone. If you know that bills need to get paid, pay them and watch your credit change.

Then we visited "the Farm" in Tennessee. I hate to use the dirty word commune, but it was one of the first communes. They like to call it an eco-village now, but it was one of the first. It was a bunch of Deadheads that left San Francisco and created this eco village and called it the Farm. We visited there and we're like, "Wow, there's a whole different life possible." The first two days were like, "We need to move and we need to live here. But the biggest piece of advice that I got, from this man they called Uncle, words that he said to me that stay with me to this day. He said, "Take the farm with you. I know you love it here, but take what you love here and apply it to where you are at home." And I'm not kidding, the moment I left that place, that has been like a mantra that plays in my head.

JIM: What do you think people don't understand about what it is like to be a small farmer right now?

KRISTI: There's a lot of folks who think like, oh what a great life. You know, you're home all day, you're at your house, you're in nature. But what they don't talk about is like, your fingers

Conversations with My Neighbors | 163

literally are blistered. They don't talk about how, you know, there's ticks all the time, and you might get Lyme disease and not know about it until you're so sick you can't get out of bed. They don't talk about sunburn or risk of skin cancer. They certainly don't talk about osteoporosis, arthritis, or any type of long-term pain that it causes.

When we first started the farm, I really thought that both Jerry and I would be able to do it full time. But in this current economy, he's got to work full time still and I have to do the farm. So not only is he working the farm full time, he's working a full-time off-the-farm job [as a journeyman pipe fitter]. So I'm full time at home and he's full-time work and then full time on the farm. I don't even know how he exists right now, so it's really hard.

JIM: Despite all of that, what is it that you love about farming?

KRISTI: Honestly, I love nature. I love the interconnectedness of the simple tasks I do here, and how they trickle and affect other people and how it's affecting my community. I don't ever want to leave this planet knowing I left it dirty. Like when you go to your friend's house, you want to make sure you didn't leave a mess, right? You want to help clean up. That's kind of how I feel about my time on the planet. This is the funny part. I am a control freak, so I really like to control what I'm putting in my body. And I like to control how it's grown. So when you work with Mother Nature, you kind of have to learn to let go of control. Like let her take control.

JIM: The other thing I want to ask you about is this. A lot of the people who are going to read this book live in places like Berkeley or Brooklyn and they look at a place like Western New York and they say, "Oh, it's all those crazy Trump people!" What do you think that people who live in big cities far away don't understand about this part of Western New York?

KRISTI: That there's a lot of young and tired, hardworking people who have realized that the government system is a setup. You asked me how I was when I was young. I was a little punk rock kid. I grew up on punk music. I grew up on listening to NOFX in my teenage years. And they have an album and there's this lyric, "The president's laughing because we voted for Nader." The song is called "The Idiots Are Taking Over." That would sum up my opinions of our government.

I've been referring to myself in the past four years as I want to be purple and there is no purple. We have Donald Trump and we have Joe Biden. Unfortunately, we have two very old dudes, which they might have some good points in and of themselves, but no, I can't even say that right now. I have such a sad distaste for our government at the moment. I'm a Bernie girl through and through. I couldn't be more thrilled to wake up this morning and finally hear Bernie speak out about what's going on in the world nowadays, and the current [Gaza] genocide we're living in. I felt like a weight was lifted off my chest to have somebody say that.

JIM: And you live in an area full of avid Trump supporters. How does that work for you?

KRISTI: Well, the thing that I would say a lot of folks don't understand about here is that in Western New York you rub shoulders with a MAGA hat person. I mean, at least for me. My father in law, for example, is a Trump guy. He'll wear a Second Amendment hat and tell me all about Fox News, and I'll laugh. I'll brush it off, and we continue on with our lives. So I think that we have a superpower around here to be able to come together and look at ourselves as people from Western New York.

My first case in point is the Buffalo Bills. Nobody gives a hoot about what's on your hat when you're in that stadium, unless it's not a Buffalo Bills hat. Because when everybody's in there, they're together, they're the Bills Mafia. Who cares? So the magical thing about this area is that we can unify and find a common ground. We can coexist with one another without wanting to rip our heads off.

Take Jon the woodman [Jon Hotaling, who is both a neighbor and fellow vendor at the Lockport Market]. Jon and I don't have a lot of the same political opinions. But I can tell you, two Saturdays ago, he brought a sweet little turtle [figurine] over to my table because he remembered that I like turtles. He saw one when he was at an estate sale. So he picked it up and he just thought, you know, I know Kristi likes turtles. And he brought it over and put it on my farmer's market stand and there it is. So this is somebody who I probably wouldn't agree with politically on a lot of things, but he thinks of me in his life.

Life in Western New York is for the hardy. You have to be a hardy breed of individual to handle the four seasons that we see here. And since we have that solidarity at the end of the day, weather, sports, and food will unite us. It's true, everybody around here is eager for summer, for either sports, the good weather, or the fact there's going to be good food around. I know that my role is the last one. I'm going to get people excited about good local food, and that's something that can bring us together. It's that interconnectivity, that little ripple that I was talking about that I like in farming. The little things I do here on a daily basis will affect that community. And hopefully if we're all not able to see eye to eye, we can all agree that I grow cool tomatoes.

Conclusion

In November 2024, Donald Trump was elected president once again. And once again people in the liberal bastions of the country asked: Who are these people in small town and rural America who have given Trump his political base and who have returned him once more to the White House? That question seemed even more important this time around. This time Trump had won with a narrow plurality of the popular vote, and political pundits were talking about a long-term political realignment, one rooted in communities just like this one in Western New York.

For more than seven years now, Lockport has been my family's home. Here is where we raised our youngest daughter through four years of high school. Here is where I became a grandfather. Here is where I ride my bicycle, buy my vegetables, swing children in the park, stand in line for ice cream, read to first graders, and shop at the hardware store. This is where I live my life now.

What have I learned here in my role of liberal outsider, weekly columnist, and citizen who calls local officials to account? What have I learned here that has wider value?

The temptation at the end of a book like this is to offer up some grand theory of the nation's politics or some grand strategy about how to make things different. There is no shortage of such theories and analyses out there at the moment, most from political pundits who have never lived in a place like this one.

That is not what I have to offer here at the end. What I have instead are three reflections from my own experience, lessons that I do believe have wider value beyond just the water's edge of the Erie Canal. They are all, at their heart, about what it takes to connect across the great national divide in this hard moment. They are about what it takes to speak "American," that lost language that lets us be fluent with people who have very different views but one powerful thing in common: a country.

Listening to How We Sound to Others

I have now written more than two hundred columns for the *Lockport Union-Sun & Journal*, on pretty much every issue facing the country and our community. When I look back on my earliest columns I cringe at my tone deafness. I spoke the standard language of the political left in America, and it was completely off key here. One of the most important things we need to do if we want to communicate with people who see the world differently is to hear how we sound through their ears.

That is the real benefit of living and writing in a small community. You hear from people. Close friends of mine write for the *New York Times*. They have a readership a thousand times larger than that of the Lockport paper, but they don't run into people in bars who tell them what they think about what they have written.

One lesson from that is about learning to listen to the strong feelings people have about an issue and to acknowledge those feelings right from the start. As I wrote about Lockport's facial recognition cameras, both locally and nationally, I always began by explaining that I had a daughter at the high school and that I cared as much about school security as anyone. Many people have real worries about school safety and speaking to that made it easier for them to hear my criticisms of the system.

When I write about guns now, I acknowledge the reasonableness of people owning guns for hunting or personal safety, then I talk about AR-15s. When I write about abortion, I recognize that many people have strong moral views about when life begins, then I make my point that they have no right to use the coercive powers of government to impose those views on other people. This may not make any converts among the true believers, but it signals to everyone else that you are at least listening to others and because of that it might be worth listening to you.

Learning about my own tone deafness also helped me spot it in others. I found a spectacular example recently in a letter to the Lockport newspaper from the Sierra Club on the subject of climate change. The letter began,

"Climate conversations often get mired in mindless money minutiae . . . as if it was possible to put a price on civilization." That rhetoric probably sounded terrific to the activists who wrote it, but here it was just a recipe for alienating people.

People struggling to pay for gas to get to work do not think of rising gas prices as "mindless money minutiae." Families worried about the price of milk aren't thinking about the "price of civilization." There are ways to reach people here on issues like this, but it is not by preaching in the language activists use with one another.

Smart advocacy is not an act of self-expression. It is an act of persuasion and that requires listening. I see similar blind spots over and over again in national politics, as progressives misread how people in working-class communities like these see some of the causes they champion.

A good example was President Biden's effort to cancel $400 billion worth of student debt (a move later blocked by the US Supreme Court). Supporters of the plan thought it was brilliant working-class politics. They said it would provide relief to students from lower-income families who went to college as a way to move up the economic ladder. They thought working-class voters would love it.

That is not the reaction I heard here. What I heard, repeatedly, was some version of, "Hey, I made the choice not to go to college because it was too expensive. Those people made a different choice. Now they think it is my responsibility to pay off their loans, seriously?"

Proposals to tax the rich also land differently here than their proponents think they will. Taxing the nation's billionaires was supposed to be a working-class winner. But when I wrote columns supporting new taxes on the wealthy, I heard back comments like, "No poor person ever gave me a job." For Markus Campbell, the Chevy salesman and swing voter, "the rich" does not conjure up images of Jeff Bezos or Elon Musk. It means Mike Smith, the General Motors dealer who has given him jobs since he was fifteen and who gave his father a job before that. He is not interested in raising taxes on the man who gives him his employment, nor are many people like him.

I have come to understand that a good portion of the popular resentment on these issues is because progressive activists and politicians spend so much time in echo chambers of the like-minded that many have lost the ability to hear how we sound to people who do not see the world in the same way we do.

Talking Much More About the Things We Love in Common

As I was wrapping up the writing of this book I was invited to speak at an event called the Lockport Lenten Luncheon. Attendees are served a meal from a popular Italian restaurant and hear a talk from some prominent member of the community. The organizers decided that the strange outsider with a column in the newspaper might make a good speaker. So on a cold day in late winter, I pedaled my bicycle across town to the local Methodist Church and found more than seventy people lined up to hear me.

I used my talk to share some of what I had learned here. One of those lessons began with retelling the blueberries story I had told at a community rally at the shuttered coal power plant by the lake. I explained how a simple tale about a granddaughter, a farm, and a tiny mouth stuffed with blueberries opened up a connection with people in a conservative rural community where I could not have been more of an outsider. I told them that my lesson that afternoon was about the importance of talking a lot more about the things we love in common, especially in a time of so much shouting over where we disagree.

I love Lockport and am genuinely grateful to be here. That is something I express often and purposefully in my columns in the newspaper. I write about the people that I admire here, about the places and pieces of local culture that I enjoy, and about simple day-to-day things like walking my granddaughter to the school bus. These are joys that we share in common as a community. These are points of connection that are deeper than our politics. I have found that writings like these give me a certain license with people to also write about the problems here, to call out politicians, and to generally be a bit of a pot stirrer.

It is easy to see how talking more about what we love in common might work at a local level where we all share a common community. But I think it is also something that has relevance for the country as a whole.

One of the widest gaps in America right now is in our comfort in even saying that we love our country. This is a point of real division. In small towns and rural communities like these, that love of country is expressed openly. It is spoken in the language of flags hanging on front porches, parades for Memorial Day and the Fourth of July, and in giant posters of local veterans hanging from lampposts. In more liberal parts of America these kinds of unvarnished expressions of love of country are harder to find.

There are many reasons for that. One is the relentless effort by political forces on the far right to try to make the national symbols of flag and anthem their own, as if they belonged only to people with their point of view. I think this has created a certain shunning of those symbols by more progressive people and places. Flying two giant American flags on the back of your pickup truck every day has become more of a partisan act than an act of patriotism.

It was notable in 2024 that Vice President Kamala Harris regularly declared in her campaign speeches, "We love our country, yes we do." It marked an important shift in the discourse coming from progressive corners. Progressive activists and communities in America are more inclined to express their patriotism in the American tradition of calling on the nation to live up to its founding promises of "liberty and justice for all." That form of love of country is spoken in the language of Henry David Thoreau, Frederick Douglass, the Suffragettes, the Civil Rights Movement, and others. Calling on the nation to be its better self and hanging a flag on a front porch are both expressions of love of country in their own way, but we have a hard time seeing that.

If you look closely, across many current issues, it is still possible to see the thing we love in common even when we seem utterly at odds. If you are a young climate activist in New York City, you may see massive solar fields on land hundreds of miles away as a sign of progress and hope. If you are a farmer like Margaret Darroch, living in a rural community targeted for a solar project larger than fifteen hundred NFL football fields, what you see is a massive industrial invasion of farmland that is open and green and used to grow food. Yet both sides are expressing love of the same thing: the environment and the Earth. I still believe there is a valuable, untapped conversation to be had there. I think that there are all kinds of things that we love in common that we do not speak of in that way nearly enough.

An Ideology of Common Sense

I think that most people in America tend to be pretty practical about things. I think that is particularly true in this part of Western New York, a place where most people work hard every day doing very practical things. They are roofers, nurses, cashiers, gardeners, furnace technicians, haircutters, and cooks. A lot of the work they do is the kind that makes the body ache after a long shift and often pays poor wages. That doesn't leave a lot of room for fluffy debate about political issues, to the extent that people think about political issues at all.

While the noise of politics comes mostly from the people who have entrenched agendas (and there is certainly a good deal of racism and backward thinking to be found here), what I have found most is that people seem to be drawn to practical solutions and common sense.

The people who I have come to know here are not dead set against immigrants, for example. What they do want are rules around immigration that are respected: How many immigrants? How will they be settled here? How will the costs be covered? As Markus Campbell told me, "I wish everybody would just come in the door and fill out the paperwork. I feel like if I was going somewhere I would have to go and fill out paperwork."

You don't hear many immigration proposals that are clear on those points. There is a certain hunger here for basic common sense in politics and this is what it sounds like. But in its absence people become supporters of policies far more draconian, offered by leaders who don't want to solve a problem but want to exploit it for their own gain.

I have found in my own writing and activism that if you tell a compelling story, grounded in factual accuracy and common sense, and if you repeat it over and over again, it has a way of finding its audience. Is that still even possible at the level of the nation, one bombarded by relentless spin? Is there a lane for common sense? I still think it is worth a shot. It is the very fact that common sense sounds so different than partisan spin that sometimes it has a chance to break through.

The Last Word

In my twenty years in Bolivia I got accustomed to living every day in a culture that was deep, rich, and not my own. I was an outsider, an alien life form in every interaction I had. Maybe after two decades away I was destined to feel like an outsider in America no matter where we landed. But when we moved from Bolivia to Lockport, I did feel like I was swapping being an outsider in one place for being a different kind of outsider in another.

I'm not sure when that changed. Was it having grandchildren here? Was it finding a local purpose as a writer and citizen? Or was it Lockport and the people here who made me feel like I still had a home in America after being so long away?

As I was circulating plans for this book to friends to solicit their feedback, a wise editor friend of mine told me, "You are still writing about

Lockport as if you are an astronaut visiting Mars. Jim, you are a Martian now."

Am I a Lockportian now, or am I some strange hybrid species? Some days my life is as locally grounded as a bicycle ride to the Erie Canal or reading to the children in the elementary school classroom of my granddaughter, Bella. Then at other times I travel to places like Kathmandu to lead an advocacy workshop for UNICEF.

I think that the coolest app on my iPhone is the Google Map. With a few movements of my fingers, I can zoom in as close as my street in Lockport or as wide as the whole planet. What other invention lets us alter our perspective in such a profound way so easily? I have come to understand that these two views of the world—one zoomed in on our day-to-day lives and the other zoomed out toward big theories—are just one more example of different sides of the same elephant, each important and valid in its own way. It was an accident for me to end up here as I moved into becoming old. I am grateful to have this chance to know the other side of the elephant and to live in this raucous and proud city with a two-century-old elevator for boats and an up-close view of the great American divide.

Notes

Chapter One

1. Arthur Pound, *The Turning Wheel; The story of General Motors through Twenty-five Years, 1908–1933* (Garden City, New York: Doubleday, Doran & Company, Inc., 1934), 467. https://archive.org/stream/turningwheelstor00pounrich/turningwheelstor00pounrich_djvu.txt.

2. Doron P. Levin, "General Motors to Cut 70,000 Jobs; 21 Plants to Shut," *New York Times*, December 19, 1991, https://www.nytimes.com/1991/12/19/business/general-motors-to-cut-70000-jobs-21-plants-to-shut.html.

3. "Quick Facts: Lockport city, New York," United States Census Bureau, accessed April 26, 2024, https://www.census.gov/quickfacts/fact/table/lockportcitynewyork/PST045222.

4. "PCBs and Lead to be removed from Eighteen Mile Creek Superfund Site in Lockport, N.Y.," Environmental Protection Agency, last modified January 31, 2017, https://www.epa.gov/archive/epa/newsreleases/pcbs-and-lead-be-removed-eighteen-mile-creek-superfund-site-lockport-ny.html.

Chapter Two

1. Anna Mehler Paperny, "Culture of Scandalous Spending," *The Globe and Mail*, September 1, 2009, https://www.theglobeandmail.com/news/national/culture-of-scandalous-spending/article4284446/.

2. Thomas J. Prohaska, "Lockport schools turn to state-of-the-art technology to beef up security," *Buffalo News*, May 20, 2018, https://buffalonews.com/news/local/education/lockport-schools-turn-to-state-of-the-art-technology-to-beef-up-security/article_7fe58b97-4f24-5a90-a408-33810f00a194.html.

3. Drew Harwell, "Unproven Facial-Recognition Companies Target Schools, Promising an End to Shootings," *Washington Post*, June 7, 2018, https://www.

washingtonpost.com/business/economy/unproven-facial-recognition-companies-target-schools-promising-an-end-to-shootings/2018/06/07/1e9e6d52-68db-11e8-9e38-24e693b38637_story.html.

4. Kashmir Hill, "Another Arrest, and Jail Time, Due to a Bad Facial Recognition Match," *New York Times*, December 29, 2020, https://www.nytimes.com/2020/12/29/technology/facial-recognition-misidentify-jail.html.

5. Connor Hoffman, "NYCLU Raps School District's Security Push," *Lockport Union-Sun & Journal*, June 27, 2019, https://www.lockportjournal.com/news/local_news/nyclu-raps-school-districts-security-push/article_8b1aec5d-b8e6-52cc-b7d2-d324b6e86745.html.

6. Chris Mills Rodrigo, "New York Suspends Facial Recognition Use in Schools," *The Hill*, December 22, 2020, https://thehill.com/policy/technology/531350-new-york-suspends-facial-recognition-use-in-schools/.

7. Thomas J. Prohaska, "State Launches Audit of Lockport Schools After Parent Complaint over Security System," *Buffalo News*, March 5, 2021, https://buffalonews.com/news/local/education/state-launches-audit-of-lockport-schools-after-parent-complaint-over-security-system/article_41bc1644-7c2f-11eb-9ace-032b9e4a317f.html.

Chapter Three

1. Eva M. Doyle, "Eva Doyle: A flight for freedom on Erie Canal," *The Buffalo News*, February 1, 2020, https://buffalonews.com/opinion/eva-doyle-a-flight-for-freedom-on-erie-canal/article_99fba193-6c1d-534a-a62e-89610d19a8c2.html.

2. "Report on the Investigation in the Death of Troy Hodge," Office of the New York State Attorney General, accessed April 29, 2024, https://ag.ny.gov/sites/default/files/oag_report_-_hodge.pdf.

3. Tim Fenster, "Demanding answers in death of Troy Hodge," *Lockport Union-Sun & Journal*, June 19, 2019, https://www.lockportjournal.com/news/local_news/demanding-answers-in-death-of-troy-hodge/article_c35b21c7-921b-515f-b98f-ff55dd56c834.html.

4. "Lockport City School District, NY," Census Reporter, accessed April 27, 2024, https://censusreporter.org/profiles/97000US3617670-lockport-city-school-district-ny/.

5. Benjamin Joe, "State ed official meets with community on My Brother's Keeper grant concerns," *Lockport Union-Sun & Journal*, August 12, 2021, https://www.lockportjournal.com/news/local_news/state-ed-official-meets-with-community-on-my-brothers-keeper-grant-concerns/article_dcf93601-a13c-5961-8c1b-b31542d322c8.html.

6. Nicholas Fandos and Jesse McKinley, "N.Y. Republican Drops Re-election Bid After Bucking His Party on Guns," *The New York Times*, June 3, 2022, https://www.nytimes.com/2022/06/03/nyregion/chris-jacobs-congress-guns.html.

7. Connor Hoffman, "Dozens attend vigil marking death of Troy Hodge in Lockport," *Lockport Union-Sun & Journal,* June 17, 2020, https://www.lockportjournal.com/news/local_news/dozens-attend-vigil-marking-death-of-troy-hodge-in-lockport/article_78da2812-cf30-5a8f-bb0a-4af8bef73dcf.html.

8. "Attorney General James' Special Investigations and Prosecutions Unit Releases Report on Investigation Into the Death of Troy Hodge," Office of the New York State Attorney General, last modified March 19, 2021, https://ag.ny.gov/press-release/2021/attorney-general-james-special-investigations-and-prosecutions-unit-releases-1.

Chapter Four

1. "Apex Appoints Ken Young to Chief Executive Officer," Apex Clean Energy, last modified July 28, 2023, https://www.apexcleanenergy.com/news/apex-appoints-ken-young-to-chief-executive-officer/.

2. "Some Reasons Why Save Ontario Shores Opposes Apex's Lighthouse Wind Industrial Turbine Project," Lake Ontario Turbines, accessed April 27, 2024, https://lakeontarioturbines.com/why-we-oppose/.

3. "Talking Points," Lake Ontario Turbines, accessed April 27, 2024, https://lakeontarioturbines.com/sos-resource-documents/#talkingpoints.

4. "Newsletters & Official Letters," Lake Ontario Turbines, accessed April 27, 2024, https://lakeontarioturbines.com/newsletters-official-letters/.

5. "The Energy to Lead: 2015 New York State Energy Plan," New York State.gov, accessed April 27, 2024, https://energyplan.ny.gov/.

6. Anne Barnard and Grace Ashford, "Can New York Really Get to 100% Clean Energy by 2040?," *New York Times,* November 29, 2021, https://www.nytimes.com/2021/11/29/nyregion/hochul-electrical-grid-climate-change.html.

7. "Niagara Falls FAQ," NYFalls, accessed April 27, 2024, https://nyfalls.com/niagara-falls/faq-4/#much.

8. John D'Onofrio, "Town residents state their case against a solar panel farm," *Lockport Union-Sun & Journal,* April 22, 2021, https://www.lockportjournal.com/news/local_news/town-residents-state-their-case-against-a-solar-panel-farm/article_c2b41c2a-a3e3-11eb-bc58-ab52802312d2.html.

9. John D'Onofrio, "Property owner addresses proposed solar project," *Lockport Union-Sun & Journal,* April 28, 2021, https://www.lockportjournal.com/news/local_news/property-owner-addresses-proposed-solar-project/article_8e623ec1-756a-549a-8220-9ddae13ab7a3.html.

10. "Ridge View solar + storage project," Ridge View Solar, accessed April 27, 2024, https://www.ridgeviewsolar.com/flipbook/1695.

11. "Bear Ridge Solar Project," Cypress Creek Renewables, accessed April 27, 2024, https://ccrenew.com/projects/bearridge/.

12. Ryan Randazzo, "Cause of APS battery explosion that injured 9 first responders detailed in new report," *AZ Central*, July 27, 2020, https://www.azcentral.com/story/money/business/energy/2020/07/27/aps-battery-explosion-surprise-new-report-findings/5523361002/.

13. "Smoke Pours from Northern NY Solar Farm Battery Blaze; Governor Says It 'may Pose Health Risks,'" *Associated Press*, July 27, 2023, https://apnews.com/article/solar-farm-batteries-fire-new-york-smoke-warning-aa10cba9cea60f2271a6fb88ea9e8697.

14. "NYPA Generating Facilities," NY Power Authority, accessed April 27, 2024, https://www.nypa.gov/power/generation/all-generating-facilities.

15. Paul Schnell, "EULOGY FOR KING COAL: The Senseless Shuttering of Somerset Station," *Lockport Union-Sun & Journal*, April 5, 2020, https://www.lockportjournal.com/news/local_news/eulogy-for-king-coal-the-senseless-shuttering-of-somerset-station/article_a9cdb21b-09a6-5265-9f56-a11b3be37fdf.html.

16. Joshua Berman, "Going Coal-Free and Clean in the Empire State," Sierra Club, last modified January 20, 2016, https://www.sierraclub.org/planet/2016/01/going-coal-free-and-clean-empire-state.

17. Tim Fenster, "Sierra Club says it supports Lighthouse Wind project," *Lockport Union-Sun & Journal*, November 1, 2018, https://www.lockportjournal.com/news/local_news/sierra-club-says-it-supports-lighthouse-wind-project/article_78f77353-c8fb-5825-bd3a-25a234367d36.html.

18. "Lake Mariner," Terawulf, accessed April 27, 2024, https://www.terawulf.com/lake-mariner-mining/.

19. "An Overview of Terawulf's Facilities," Terawulf, accessed April 27, 2024, https://www.terawulf.com/terawulf-facilities/.

20. Benjamin Joe, "Somerset data center gets approval," *Lockport Union-Sun & Journal*, August 7, 2021, https://www.lockportjournal.com/news/local_news/somerset-data-center-gets-approval/article_3c4c4feb-2df6-53d1-a428-5c725adedb59.html.

21. C. Mandler, "New York becomes the first state to ban gas stoves in new residential construction," *CBS News*, May 3, 2023, https://www.cbsnews.com/news/new-york-ban-gas-stoves-new-residential-construction/.

22. Eric D. Lebel, Colin J. Finnegan, Zutao Ouyang, and Robert B. Jackson, "Methane and NO_x Emissions from Natural Gas Stoves, Cooktops, and Ovens in Residential Homes," *Environmental Science & Technology* 56, no. 4 (February 2022), 2529-2539, https://doi.org/10.1021/acs.est.1c04707.

23. "Gas stoves are even worse for the climate than previously thought, study shows," *CBS News*, January 28, 2022, https://www.cbsnews.com/news/climate-change-gas-stoves-methane-study/.

24. Ari Natter, "US Safety Agency to Consider Ban on Gas Stoves Amid Health Fears," *Bloomberg*, January 9, 2023, https://www.bloomberg.com/news/articles/2023-01-09/us-safety-agency-to-consider-ban-on-gas-stoves-amid-health-fears?leadSource=uverify%20wall.

25. Ella Nilsen and Rachel Ramirez, "New York Becomes the First State to Ban Natural Gas Stoves and Furnaces in Most New Buildings," *CNN*, May 3, 2023, https://www.cnn.com/2023/05/03/us/new-york-natural-gas-ban-climate?cid=ios_app.

26. "Senator Rob Ortt & Western New Yorkers Say No to Albany's Gas Stove Ban," New York State Senate, last modified January 20, 2023, https://www.nysenate.gov/newsroom/press-releases/2023/robert-g-ortt/senator-rob-ortt-western-new-yorkers-say-no-albanys-gas.

27. C. Mandler, "New York Becomes the First State to Ban Gas Stoves in New Residential Construction." CBS News report, May 3, 2023 https://www.cbsnews.com/news/new-york-ban-gas-stoves-new-residential-construction/.

28. Nate McMurray (@Nate_McMurray), "It's not propaganda. People need gas stoves. The storm kind of showed us that, especially considering how horrible our infrastructure is in western New York," Twitter, April 30, 2023, https://twitter.com/Nate_McMurray/status/1652681879034658819.

29. Jim Shultz, "Climate Change on the Ballot," The Democracy Center, accessed April 27, 2024, https://static1.squarespace.com/static/5e49ea5f94c2c44a94262103/t/5e6c3614f26ba22b9941d266/1584150122958/Proposition_23.pdf.

Chapter Five

1. Sam Roberts, "Infamous 'Drop Dead' Was Never Said by Ford," *New York Times*, December 28, 2006, https://www.nytimes.com/2006/12/28/nyregion/28veto.html.

2. Emanual Perlmutter, "City Starts Promoting Betting Service," *New York Times*, December 30, 1970, https://www.nytimes.com/1970/12/30/archives/city-starts-promoting-betting-service.html?searchResultPosition=1.

3. "Western Regional Off Track Betting 2021 Annual Report," Western Regional Off Track Betting, accessed April 27, 2024, https://www.westernotb.com/wp-content/uploads/2022/08/2021-Annual-Report.pdf.

4. "Western Regional OTB returns over $250 Million to Local Governments!," Western Regional Off Track Betting, accessed April 27, 2024, https://www.westernotb.com/returns-millions/.

5. Philip Gambini, "County Legislature Turns Back OTB Audit Call," *Lockport Union-Sun & Journal*, May 7, 2019, https://www.lockportjournal.com/news/local_news/county-legislature-turns-back-otb-audit-call/article_9c0d5769-f501-506e-9008-c7eab49857e4.html.

6. Jim Heaney and Philip Gambini, "Lawyers Tell OTB to Ditch the Perks," *Investigative Post*, May 16, 2019, https://www.investigativepost.org/2019/05/16/lawyers-tell-otb-to-ditch-the-perks/.

7. "Western Regional Off-Track Betting Corporation—Marketing and Promotional Program (2021 M-65)," Office of the New York State Comptroller,

last modified September 23, 2021, https://www.osc.ny.gov/local-government/audits/off-track-betting/2021/09/23/western-regional-off-track-betting-corporation-marketing-and#:~:text=The%20Corporation%20was%20formed%20as,cities%20of%20Buffalo%20and%20Rochester.

8. Quotes from Michael Nolan are from an interview with the author on December 21, 2021.

9. Quotes from Phil Barnes are from an interview with the author on January 13, 2022.

10. Matthew Spina, "State Comptroller Criticizes OTB over Perks for Board Members, Executives," *Buffalo News*, September 23, 2021, https://buffalonews.com/news/local/government-and-politics/state-comptroller-criticizes-otb-over-perks-for-board-members-executives/article_3ed7b8f4-1c91-11ec-911d-43a279f2c0d1.html.

11. Mike Pettinella, "Genesee's WROTB Director Addresses Recent Issues," *The Batavian*, October 11, 2021, https://www.thebatavian.com/mike-pettinella/genesees-wrotb-director-addresses-recent-issues/573318.

12. "Highmark Stadium Suites," Suite Experience Group, accessed April 27, 2024, https://www.suiteexperiencegroup.com/all-suites/highmark-stadium/.

13. Jim Heaney, "OTB's Part-time Board Enjoys Gold-Plated Perks," *Investigative Post*, December 4, 2018, https://www.investigativepost.org/2018/12/04/otbs-part-time-board-enjoys-gold-plated-perks/.

14. Heaney, "OTB's Part-Time Board Enjoys Gold-Plated Perks."

15. Kathryn Sheingold, "Informal Opinion No. 2008-3," Office of the New York State General, https://ag.ny.gov/sites/default/files/opinions/I_2008-3_pw.pdf.

16. "Amherst Police seek male suspect in OTB armed robbery," *WGRZ*, August 28, 2021, https://www.wgrz.com/article/news/crime/amherst-police-seeking-male-suspect-in-off-track-betting-armed-robbery/71-382fdddd-5084-48bc-8a70-1d11308c5cdd.

17. Pettinella, "Genesee's WROTB Director Addresses Recent Issues."

18. Pettinella, "Genesee's WROTB Director Addresses Recent Issues."

19. Susanne Craig, Thomas Kaplan, and William K. Rashbaum, "After Ethics Panel's Shutdown, Loopholes Live on in Albany," *New York Times*, December 8, 2014, https://www.nytimes.com/2014/12/08/nyregion/after-moreland-commission-shutdown-by-gov-cuomo-loopholes-live-on-in-albany.html?mcubz=1.

20. Patrick Lakamp, "State Pays Lancaster Woman in Sex Harassment Settlement," *Buffalo News*, October 5, 2012, https://buffalonews.com/news/state-pays-lancaster-woman-in-sex-harassment-settlement/article_97ceaf90-b59d-5e4a-8259-e5df654f2b17.html.

21. Thomas J. Prohaska, "Former Maziarz Aide Aronow Receives Niagara County Job," *Buffalo News*, January 15, 2020, https://buffalonews.com/news/local/former-maziarz-aide-aronow-receives-niagara-county-job/article_badd8802-bd53-50a5-a99d-9a4dd598ef61.html.

22. Robert McCarthy and Matthew Spina, "FBI Examining Contracts at Western Regional OTB," *Buffalo News*, April 29, 2019, https://buffalonews.com/business/local/fbi-examining-contracts-at-western-regional-otb/article_a44fd00d-4859-5af4-a0d6-1a841895ef43.html.

23. J. Dale Shoemaker, "OTB Shells Out Millions for Lawyers and Lobbyists," *Investigative Post*, October 19, 2023, https://www.investigativepost.org/2023/10/19/otb-shells-out-millions-for-lawyers-and-lobbyists/.

24. Quotes from Dennis Virtuoso are from an interview with the author on January 27, 2022.

25. "DiNapoli Audit Finds Western Regional OTB Lacks Accountability and Gave Out Lucrative Perks," Office of the New York State Comptroller, last modified September 23, 2021, https://www.osc.ny.gov/press/releases/2021/09/dinapoli-audit-finds-western-regional-otb-lacks-accountability-and-gave-out-lucrative-perks.

26. "DiNapoli Audit Finds Western Regional OTB Lacks Accountability and Gave Out Lucrative Perks," Office of the New York State Comptroller.

27. Philip Gambini and Rick Pfeiffer, "Maziarz airs bid-rigging claims," *Lockport Union-Sun & Journal*, February 27, 2019, https://www.lockportjournal.com/news/local_news/maziarz-airs-bid-rigging-claims/article_6782daa6-2c72-520a-812b-23c8bd0f9d6f.html.

28. Mark Scheer, "Maziarz sues OTB alleging 'fraud,'" *Lockport Union-Sun & Journal*, May 12, 2022, https://www.lockportjournal.com/maziarz-sues-otb-alleging-fraud/article_091a07ed-06df-5038-88cc-64f5180ff900.html.

29. Jim Heaney, "OTB's part-time board enjoys gold-plated perks," *Investigative Post*, December 4, 2018, https://www.investigativepost.org/2018/12/04/otbs-part-time-board-enjoys-gold-plated-perks/.

30. Matthew Spina, "Former executive sues Western Regional OTB, says he was fired for cooperated with FBI," *The Buffalo News*, August 14, 2021, https://buffalonews.com/online/former-executive-sues-western-regional-otb-says-he-was-fired-for-cooperating-with-fbi/article_ff313732-fd34-11eb-b314-634b2e23d2be.html.

31. Gambini, "County Legislature Turns Back OTB Audit Call."

32. Benjamin Joe, "OTB, campaign finance resolutions sent to committee," *Lockport Union-Sun & Journal*, October 19, 2021, https://www.lockportjournal.com/news/local_news/otb-campaign-finance-resolutions-sent-to-committee/article_fae2b40d-28b1-5a07-8f0f-3eb0194538ca.html.

33. Mark Scheer, "OTB Reform Bills Pass First Test," *Investigative Post*, February 14, 2022, https://www.investigativepost.org/2022/02/14/otb-reform-bills-pass-first-test/.

34. Jim Heaney, "OTB Tries to Stifle a Critic," *Investigative Post*, June 6, 2022, https://www.investigativepost.org/2022/06/06/otb-tries-to-stifle-a-critic/.

35. Ryan Whalen, "Big Changes to Western Regional Off-Track Betting Corporation Board Structure Included in Final Budget Bill," *Spectrum News*, May 2,

2023, https://spectrumlocalnews.com/nys/central-ny/politics/2023/05/02/big-changes-to-western-regional-otb-board-structure-included-in-final-budget-bill.

 36. Niagara County Legislature, *6-20-23 Meeting Minutes*, accessed April 27, 2024, https://cms5.revize.com/revize/niagaracounty/Document_center/Department/G-L/Legislature/Agenda%20&%20Minutes/6-20-23%20MEETING%20MINUTES.pdf.

 37. J. Dale Shoemaker and Geoff Kelly, "Big Shakeup at the Besieged OTB," *Investigative Post*, May 3, 2023, https://www.investigativepost.org/2023/05/03/big-shakeup-at-the-besieged-otb/.

 38. Mark Scheer, "Contract Extensions for 18 OTB Executives," *Investigative Post*, July 10, 2023, https://www.investigativepost.org/2023/07/10/contract-extensions-for-18-otb-executives/.

 39. Scheer, "Contract Extensions for 18 OTB Executives."

 40. Geoff Kelly and J. Dale Shoemaker, "Plan Would See Byron Brown Succeed Henry Wojtaszek at Western Regional OTB," *Lockport Union-Sun & Journal*, February 6, 2024, https://www.lockportjournal.com/news/plan-would-see-byron-brown-succeed-henry-wojtaszek-at-western-regional-otb/article_2d918125-e455-5ce2-b10b-17787e38e0a0.html.

About the Author

Born and raised in Whittier California, President Richard Nixon's hometown, Jim reacted by becoming a progressive political activist as a teenager. After graduating from UC Berkeley, he spent twenty years deeply involved in California politics—as staff to the California Legislature and as a consumer advocate, with a detour to Harvard University for a graduate degree along the way. In the early 1990s, Jim and his wife, Lynn Nesselbush, spent their first year of marriage as volunteers in an orphanage in Cochabamba, Bolivia. They later returned, living there for nineteen years. Bolivia is also where they met and adopted their three children, Elizabeth, Miguel and Mariana. As founder and executive director of the Democracy Center for three decades, Jim has led and won advocacy campaigns from the local level to the global and has trained and supported citizen activists across five continents. He currently serves as a global advocacy advisor to UNICEF, as faculty at UC Berkeley and the Salzburg Seminar, and as a contributing writer at *New York Review*. He and Lynn now reside in Lockport, New York across the street from their two eldest granddaughters.

Other Books by Jim Shultz

The Initiative Cookbook: Recipes and Stories from California's Ballot Wars
The Democracy Owners' Manual: A Practical Guide to Changing the World
Dignity and Defiance: Stories from Bolivia's Challenge to Globalization
My Other Country: Nineteen Years in Bolivia
The Art of Advocacy Strategy

Index

abortion, 130, 150, 168
Alba, Davy (*New York Times* reporter), 38–39
Alexander-Minter, Rae, 65–67
Alston, Anael (New York Department of Education's Assistant Commissioner for Access, Equity, and Community Engagement Services), 62, 64
American Dream, the, 136, 138–139
Apex Clean Energy, 77, 92. *See also* power, renewable: wind energy
Aronow, Glenn (Western Regional Off-Track Betting contractor), 109
Atwater, Pam, 76–78
Atwater, Randy, 87–88

Baes, Gene, 100, 146–151
Barclay Damon law firm, 112
Barnes, Phil (Western Regional Off-Track Betting Board Member), 105, 109, 110, 112–113
Barrett, Anna (Lockport High School teacher), 69
Batavia Downs Gaming, racetrack, and casino, 102–104, 107, 110, 121, 123–124, 160
Beauchamp, Alex (Food & Water Watch regional director), 96–97
Beowulf Energy, 93

Betsch, Raymond (Lockport Mayor), 133
betting parlors. *See* Off-Track Betting (OTB)
Bianchi, Richard (Western Regional Off-Track Betting Chairman), 105, 112–113
Biden, Jill, 68
Biden, Joe, xi, 68, 150, 165, 169
bitcoin mining, 95. *See also* power, renewable; Lake Mariner Data Center; *Lockport Union-Sun & Journal*: in favor of data center; TeraWulf Corporation
Bittner, Jim, 87
Black population in Lockport: desegregating public schools, 66; on facial recognition surveillance cameras, 40, 42; history of, 2, 4, 52, 65–67, 132; on My Brother's Keeper program, 61–65, 69; neighborhood with significant portion of, 51; newspaper columns on, 55–60; on Troy Hodge's death, 53–55, 58–60, 72; underrepresentation in government agencies, 7, 31, 43–44, 56, 73, 135; in a White, conservative community, 23, 51, 55–60, 63–65, 72–73, 132, 145–146, 172

Bonito, Marissa (Lockport Police officer), 72
Bradley, Michelle (District Superintendent): background of, 30; planning for My Brother's Keeper program, 61–62, 64; regarding facial recognition surveillance cameras, 25, 37, 46, 48
Brown, Byron (Western Regional Off-Track Betting President), 123
Brown, Richard (Hartland Town Planning Board member), 87
Brown vs. the Board of Topeka, 66
Buddha's story about the three blind men and elephant, the, xiv–xv, 100, 173
Buffalo, New York, 68–70, 101–102, 107, 115, 120, 138
Buffalo Bills, 6, 104–115 passim, 131, 165
Buffalo News, 36–37, 46, 50, 114, 115–116
Bush, George W., 127
Buttigieg, Pete, 129
Buzzfeed, 37

Calamita, Nicole, 53
Calvin III, Mathis (Superintendent), 49, 73
Campbell, Kevin (EDF Renewables project manager), 85, 86
Campbell, Markus (Lockport General Motors dealership manager), 125–131, 172
Caruso, Jill, 47
Casey, Steven, 123
Cauley, Kandyce, 56–59
Cheatham, Kiki, 42
Cheatham, Renee (Lockport School Board member), 41–44, 49, 61–62, 64, 67, 73

Cheatham, Ronald (Ron) (North Park Junior High School peer mediator), 41–43, 72
children's books, xii, 18–19
Citizen Advisory Committee of Lockport, 133
Civil War, United States, 6, 65–66, 158
Clayton, Tara, 64
climate activism: and messaging, 168–169, 171; backlash to, 98–100; on coal energy, 91–93, 95–96, 159; on natural gas, 96–97; on solar energy, 88; on wind energy, 77–78
climate change, 14–15, 85, 93–100 passim, 125, 151, 168–169. *See also* climate activism; power, renewable
Clinton, Hillary, 128–129
coal plant closure, 90–96, 159, 170
Coder, Deborah (Lockport School District Assistant Superintendent for Finance and Management Services), 27, 31, 44, 46
common sense in politics, 172
Confer Plastics, 125, 136–137
Confer, Bob (owner of Confer Plastics and columnist), 125, 136–141
corruption, political, xv, 101–124
COVID-19 pandemic, 43, 70, 137, 150
Coyle, Stefanie (New York Civil Liberties Union lawyer), 39–41
cryptocurrency, 94–95
Cuomo, Andrew (New York Governor), 43, 45, 91, 114, 137, 159
Cypress Creek Renewables, 85. *See also* power, renewable: solar energy

Daily News, 101
Darroch, Margaret, 79, 84–87 passim, 98, 171
data center, 93–95
Democracy Center, xv, 100

Devine, Mark (Lockport Common Councilmember), 71–72
Dickerson, Holly (Lockport School District grant writer), 63–64
DiNapoli, Thomas (New York State Comptroller), 45–46, 111, 115
Dreamers, 13–14. *See also* immigration
Drozdz, Zuzanna, 87, 89

economics in politics, xv, 160, 169
EDF Renewables, 83–85. *See also* power, renewable: solar energy
Ellis, Wright (Cambria Town Supervisor), 85
energy, renewable. *See* power, renewable
Engert, Dan (Somerset Town Supervisor), 93–94
environmentalism. *See* climate activism
Erie County, 115, 120, 138

Facebook, 38, 93, 144, 153. *See also* Lockportians Facebook group
Fendt, Charlie, 80, 82, 86
Filicetti, Michael (Niagara County Sheriff), 72
Food & Water Watch, 96
Forbes Magazine, 37
Ford, Gerald, 101
fossil fuels, 76, 91–92, 95, 96. *See also* coal plant closure; power, renewable
4-H Club, 75
Fox News, 156, 165
Floyd, George, 67, 70
Flynn, KC (SNTech founder), 26
Fugitive Slave Act, 65

gambling. *See* Off-Track Betting (OTB)
gas heating and cooking equipment, ban of; *See* power, renewable: gas heating and cooking equipment
Gasport, New York, 79, 84

General Motors in Lockport: employees of, 41, 56, 126–127, 131, 132–136, 139, 140–141, 169; history of, xiii, 3, 6, 52
Glaser, Jessica (Town of Pendelton Conservation Advisory Councilmember), 87
global warming, 14–15, 85, 93–100 passim, 125, 151, 168–169. *See also* environmentalists; power, renewable
Goldberg, William "Lefty" (Western Regional Off-Track Betting founder), 102
guns: in national politics, 130, 168. *See also* Las Vegas music festival shooting; Lockportians Facebook group; Sandy Hook Elementary School

Hardwick, Kevin (Erie County Comptroller), 110
Harris, Kamala, 68, 171
Harrison, Herbert (The Harrison Radiator Company founder), 3
Hartland Town Planning Board, 79–80, 87
Harwell, Drew (*Washington Post* writer), 37
Hawkins, Flora (Lockport Common Councilmember), 125, 131–136
Heaney, Jim (*Investigative Post* founder), 106, 114, 119, 121
Hederman, Rea (*New York Review* owner), 118
Hochul, Kathy (New York Governor), 68, 96–97
Hodge, Fatima, 52–53, 70–72
Hodge, Troy, 7, 67, 69; community reactions to the death of, 58–60; events that led to the death of, 52–55; exoneration of police officers involved in death of, 72; march

Index | 187

Hodge, Troy *(continued)*
and kneeling in memory of, 70–71, 145; mayoral response to death of, 54, 71, 141, 144–145; report from Attorney General on the death of, 71; settlement on the wrongful death of, 72, 145
Hodgson Russ law firm, 117–19
Hoffman, Connor (*Lockport Union-Sun & Journal* reporter), 22, 32–33, 35, 37, 47, 71
Holly, Birdsill Jr, .4
Horvath, Kenneth, 20
Hotaling, Jon, 156–161, 165–166
Huston, Steve, 64

immigration: conversations with neighbors about, 131, 138–139, 160–161, 172; to Lockport, 6, 18, 136, 138–139; newspaper columns about, 13–14, 15, 20. *See also* Black population in Lockport: history of; Irish population in Lockport; Italian population in Lockport
Indian Point nuclear power plant, 78
Investigative Post: on Buffalo Billions corruption scandal, 114; on lead poisoning among children of poor families in Buffalo, 114; on Western Regional Off-Track Betting corruption, 106, 110–115 passim, 119, 121–122
Irish population in Lockport, 2, 52
Italian population in Lockport, 4, 52, 132

Jacobs, Chris (United States Congressman), 70
James, Leticia (New York Attorney General), 71
Jansen, Norm (Somerset Town Planning Board chair), 95

Jastrzemski, Joseph (Niagara County Clerk), 20
Jenkins, Kimberly, 54
Joe, Benjamin (*Lockport Union-Sun & Journal* reporter), 63

Kavanaugh, Brian (New York State Senator), 44–45
Kennedy, Tim (Democratic State Senator), 115, 120, 121
Kenzie, Abby, 163
King, Will, 56, 58
Kintigh Generating Station, 90–95, 159, 170
Kowalski, Tina and Karl, 81–83, 90

Lake Mariner Data Center, 93–95
Lambalzer, Kyle (Lockport School District Board member), 35–36
Las Vegas music festival shooting, 11
Lee, Forrester, 65–67
Liberace, Władziu Valentino, 132
Lieberman, Donna (New York Civil Liberties Union executive director), 39
Lighthouse Wind, 77, 87. *See also* power, renewable: wind energy
Linderman, John (Lockport Board of Education President), 30–32
LiPuma, Robert (Lockport School District Director of Assessment & Technology), 32, 46
Lockport, City of: culture of, 5–7; Erie Canal in, xiii, 2–4, 10, 18, 21, 52, 65; history of, xiii, 1–4, 52, 65–68; landmarks of, 3–7, 8, 17, 20, 51–52; mayoral election, 20, 141–144; population of, xii–xiii, 1–7, 51; Superfund site, 4–5; town writer of, 23; transportation in, 1–4, 91. *See also* Citizens Advisory Committee of Lockport; Lockport Common

Council; Unity Music Festival of Lockport
Lockport Community Market, 7, 17–18; conversations at the, xv, 22; vendors of the, 79, 157, 161, 165–166
Lockport, Town of, 81–83
Lockport Board of Education. *See* Lockport City School District
Lockport City Hall, 54, 69–71, 111. *See also* Lockport Common Council
Lockport City School District: budget of, 35–36; desegregation of, 66; elections of school board of, 35, 43–44, 49; enrollment in, 137; funds from Smart Schools Bond Act, 25–26; governance of, 35; lawsuit against board of, 41–44; My Brother's Keeper program, 60–64, 69; new superintendent of, 48–49; racism in, 7, 42, 49, 52, 58, 73, 145; renaming junior high school in honor of Aaron Mossell, 66–68, 73. *See also* Lockport High School; North Park Junior High School; surveillance cameras, facial recognition
Lockport Common Council, 7, 53–54, 69–72, 125, 131, 133–135. *See also* Lockport City Hall
Lockport Educators' Association, 29, 34, 49, 73
Lockport High School: being Black in, 57–58; in *The New York Times*, 38–39; employees of, 35; graduates of, 1, 34, 39, 53, 55, 56, 64, 146–147; post-graduate experience, 3, 5; PTA members of, 62. *See also* Lockport City School District; surveillance cameras, facial recognition
Lockport in Bloom, 35
Lockport General Motors Plant. *See* General Motors in Lockport

Lockportians Facebook group, xiv, 11; on Donald Trump, 15–16; on guns, 12–13; on immigration, 13–14; reactions in the aftermath of Troy Hodge's death, 55, 59–60; on renewable power, 14–15; on surveillance cameras 33–34, 47–48
Lockport Police Department: board of, 132, 145; in *New York Times* 38–39; experience of Black community members with, 51, 55, 56, 59; lacking Black officers, 7. *See also* Hodge, Troy
Lockport Public Library, 40
Lockport Union-Sun & Journal: on Black community members, 55–60; on coal plant closure, 92; on data center, 93; on facial recognition surveillance cameras, 25, 31, 32–33, 35, 37, 45, 46, 47; on the first anniversary of Troy Hodge's death, 71; on Jim Shultz as a grandfather, 18–19; on Jim Shultz as "the writer," 21–23; Jim Shultz joining the, xiii, 8–11, 168; Joyce Miller joining the, 151–152; on junior high school renaming ceremony, 67; letters from readers, 59, 67–68; on local elections, 20, 44; on local life, 20–21; on the Lockport Community Market, 17; on Lockport's immigrants, 18; on My Brother's Keeper program, 62–63; on Niagara County Sheriff hiring police officer involved in Troy Hodge's death, 72; on privatization of ambulance service, 155; on solar power, 80–82, 86–87, 88–89; on Western Regional Off-Track Betting (WROTB) corruption, 114, 115, 116–117, 120, 122–123
Lombardi, Jon (Lockport Mayor), 141
Love Canal toxic waste site, 4, 89
Lutz, Darlene, 92

Marjory Stoneman Douglas High School, 36
Martin, Trayvon, 60–61
Mason, John, 92
Maziarz, George (New York State Senator), 108–109, 111, 114, 160
McCollum, Dale, 82
McDonald, Jayde, 39, 55, 57–58
McGovern, George (United States Senator), xv
McMicken, Arizona, storage battery blast, 86
McMurray, Nate (candidate for Congress), 97
Mesi, Deanna, 34
Miles, Joyce (*Lockport Union-Sun & Journal* newspaper editor): background on, 9–10; interview of, 125, 151–156; on facial recognition surveillance cameras, 28; on school board election, 44; on series on Black residents, 55; on solar power, 86; on Western Regional Off-Track Betting, 116–118
Miller, William E. (Congressman), 1
Minneapolis, 70
Morath, Joseph (attorney for Hodge family), 71
Mossell, Aaron (namesake for Lockport junior high school), 65–68, 73. *See also* Lockport City School District; North Park Junior High School
Mossell, Charles, 65
MTV News, 37–38
My Brother's Keeper program, 61–64, 69

National Public Radio (NPR), 37
National Rifle Association (NRA), 70
Neiss, James (*Lockport Union-Sun & Journal* photographer), 63
New York State Attorney General, 52, 54, 71, 106–107, 117–118

New York's State Commissioner of Education, 49
New York City financial troubles, 101
New York Civil Liberties Union (NYCLU), 27, 39–41, 43–44
New York Freedom of Information Law, 39, 114–115, 121
New York Office of Information Technology Assessment, 49
New York Review, xiv, 43, 116, 118
New York State "Big Ugly" budget process, 119–120
New York State Comptroller, 45–46, 104–106, 111, 114–115, 117–119. *See also* DiNapoli, Thomas; Hardwick, Kevin
New York State Education Department, 39, 40, 44, 45, 64
New York State Legislature, 44, 102, 122
New York State Office of Renewable Energy Siting (ORES), 88
New York Times, xiv, 38–39, 92, 168
Newman, Doug, 15–16
Niagara County, xiii, 120, 138, 141, 159–160, 161
Niagara County Fair, 75
Niagara County Sheriff, 52, 71, 72
Niagara County Solar Study Group. *See* power, renewable: solar energy
Niagara Gazette, 88, 114, 115, 121–123
Niagara Falls: City of 4, 143, 160; hydropower generation from, 79, 91, 95–96, 137; school district in, 137; waterfall of, 2. *See also* Batavia Downs Gaming
Nixon, Richard, xv
Nolan, Michael (Western Regional Off-Track Betting Chief Operating Officer), 105–107, 109, 112–113, 121
Norris, Michael (New York State Assemblyman), 97

North Park Junior High School, 42, 146–147; renaming junior high school in honor of Aaron Mossell, 66–68, 73

Oates, Joyce Carol, 1
Obama, Barack, 61, 125–129
Obat, Victoria (Lockport District School Board member), 31
Off-Track Betting (OTB), 101–124; history of, 101–102; Western Regional Off-Track Betting Corporation (WROTB) corruption, 104–124, 160
Olivo, Anthony (Tony) (security consultant), 27–29, 31–32, 34, 37–39
Ontario Lottery and Gaming Corporation, 26
Ortt, Robert (New York State Senator), 19, 97, 108–109, 111, 120
Outten, Barbara, 82

pandemic, 43, 70, 137, 150
patriotism, 170–171
payments in lieu of taxes (PILOTs), 86, 89, 159
Pease, Barbara, 20
Pease, Chris, 20
polarization, political, 154
police: funding, 33. *See also* Lockport Police Department; Niagara County Sheriff
power, renewable, 23, 75–100; community forum on solar energy, 80, 82; components to
produce, 14; gas heating and cooking equipment, ban of, 96–97, 99; hydropower, 76–79, 91, 95–96, 137; *Lockport Union-Sun & Journal* on, 80–82, 86–87; New York State goals for, 78; Niagara County Solar Study Group, 87–88; risks of solar batteries, 86; solar energy, 15, 21, 80–88, 93, 98, 171; storage batteries, electrical, 80, 86; wind energy, 14–15, 75–79 passim, 87, 92, 99
Powley, Brent, 82
Preisch, Steven (Lockport Chief of Police), 54
Prohaska, Thomas (*Buffalo News* reporter), 36–37

racism in Lockport. *See* Black population in Lockport: in a White, conservative community. *See also* Lockport City School District: racism in
racism in the United States, xv, 15, 65–66, 68, 70
Renewable Properties, 82–83
Rezarch, Frank, 20
Ridge View Solar, 80, 84, 86
Rochester, New York, 101–102, 120
Rockefeller, Nelson (New York Governor), 132
Roman, Michelle (Lockport Mayor): elections of, 20; impressions of Lockport of, 6; interview with, 125, 141–146; regarding renaming of junior high school, 67; in response to Troy Hodge's death, 54, 71; Salter Jr., Aaron, 68–70
Rotilio, Antonella (United Public Service Union representative), 107

Sanders, Bernie, 165
Sanders, Mark, 56–59, 69
Sandy Hook Elementary School, 11, 31, 36
Save Ontario Shores, 77
Saykin, Aaron M. (partner in Hodgson Russ law firm), 117–118
Scapelliti, Joseph (Lockport High School coach), 35–36

Scheer, Mark (*Niagara Gazette* reporter), 114, 121, 124
Schnell, Paul, 92
school security. *See* surveillance cameras, facial recognition
Seaton, Matt (*New York Review* editor), 116
Seuss, Dr., xii, 18
Shell Oil, 85
Sherrell, Daniel (Sierra Club organizer), 91
Shultz et al v. New York State Department of Education, 41, 43–44
Shultz, Mariana, xiii, 10, 25, 38, 53
Siebert, Richard (Western Regional Off-Track Betting Board Member), 105, 107
Sierra Club of New York, 90–92, 95–96, 168–169
Smart Schools Bond Act, 25–27, 29
SNTech, 25–26, 29, 32, 34, 38–39, 44–45
Sobieraski, Dennis, 47
spy cameras. *See* surveillance cameras, facial recognition
storage batteries, electrical. *See* power, renewable: storage batteries, electrical
story about the three blind men and elephant, xiv–xv, 100, 173
Supreme Court, 66
surveillance cameras, facial recognition, 23; audit of school district's purchase of, 45–56; national issue regarding, 36–38, 42, 49–50; lawsuit against school district for, 41–44; legislation banning, 44–45; lessons from, 90, 116, 168; local media coverage of, 25, 28–29, 32–33, 35–36; local public reaction to, 29, 33–35; privacy and, 39–40, 45; school district board meeting on, 29–32; school district's launch of, 40; school district's threats to maintain, 25–36; Smart Schools Bond Act funding for, 25–26, 27, 29; state ban of, 49; technology of, 26–27, 28–29, 38–39. *See also* Olivo, Anthony
Syracuse, John (Republican legislator), 113

teachers' union, 29, 34, 49, 73
Tenney, Claudia (New York Congresswoman), 120
TeraWulf Corporation, 94–95
Tomlinson, Javeon, 69
Tops Market, 68–70
transgender, xi–xii
Travis, Paula, 62
Trump, Donald: conversations with locals about, xiv, 125–129, 136, 139, 140, 150, 160, 164–165; Jim Shultz's articles about, xiv, 9, 10–11, 13, 15–16, 116; local support for, xiii, 1–2, 5, 8, 15–16, 33, 93, 143; national support for, xii–xiv, 5, 167; populist conservative politics and, 140; in response to Buffalo shooting, 70
turbines, wind. *See* power, renewable: wind energy
Twain, Mark, 121

Uhren, Cameron (SNTech founder), 26. *See also* SNTech
Ulrich, David, 7
Union-Sun and Journal. *See Lockport Union-Sun and Journal*
United Public Service Union, 107. *See also* Western Regional Off-Track Betting
United States Civil War, 6, 65–66, 158
United States Consumer Products Safety Commission, 96
United States Supreme Court, 66

Unity Music Festival of Lockport, 135–136
Urban Renewal, 4, 52, 132

Vice, 37
Virtuoso, Dennis (Niagara County Legislator), 110
Vizcarra, Mindy and Oscar, 84, 86

Waddy, Nicholas L., 8
Wallace, Monica (New York State Assemblywoman), 44–45, 115, 120
Washington Post, The, 37
Western Regional Off-Track Betting Corporation (WROTB). *See* Off-Track Betting (OTB)
Winquist, Jerry, 161, 163–164
Winquist, Kristi, 161–166
Winter, Elliott (Niagara County Board Representative to Western Regional Off-Track Betting), 106, 109, 123
Winter, Rick (Niagara County Representative to Western Regional Off-Track Betting), 106, 109–110
Wilson, Garth, 67
Wohleben, David (candidate for Lockport Mayor), 20
Wojtaszek, Caroline (County District Attorney), 54, 109, 112
Wojtaszek, Henry F. (Western Regional Off-Track Betting President), 108–113, 115, 116, 118–123, 160
Wydish, Rebecca (Chair of Niagara County Legislature), 113

Young, Karen (Board of Education President), 46, 63
Young, Teria, 62–63